# SOCIAL ISSUES FIRSTHAND

# Homosexuality

David M. Haugen and Matthew J. Box,
Book Editors

Bruce Glassman, Vice President
Bonnie Szumski, Publisher
Helen Cothran, Managing Editor
Scott Barbour, Series Editor

**GREENHAVEN PRESS**
*An imprint of Thomson Gale, a part of The Thomson Corporation*

Detroit • New York • San Francisco • San Diego • New Haven, Conn.
Waterville, Maine • London • Munich

© 2006 Thomson Gale, a part of The Thomson Corporation.

Thomson and Star Logo are trademarks and Gale and Greenhaven Press are registered trademarks used herein under license.

*For more information, contact*
Greenhaven Press
27500 Drake Rd.
Farmington Hills, MI 48331-3535
Or you can visit our Internet site at http://www.gale.com

Greenhaven Press anthologies primarily consist of previously published material taken from a variety of sources, including periodicals, books, scholarly journals, newspapers, government documents, and position papers from private and public organizations. These original sources are often edited for length and to ensure their accessibility for a young adult audience. The anthology editors also change the original titles of these works in order to clearly present the main thesis of each viewpoint and to explicitly indicate the opinion presented in the viewpoint. These alterations are made in consideration of both the reading and comprehension levels of a young adult audience. Every effort is made to ensure that Greenhaven Press accurately reflects the original intent of the authors included in this anthology.

**ALL RIGHTS RESERVED.**
No part of this work covered by the copyright hereon may be reproduced or used in any form or by any means—graphic, electronic, or mechanical, including photocopying, recording, taping, Web distribution or information storage retrieval systems—without the written permission of the publisher.

Every effort has been made to trace the owners of copyrighted material.

Cover credit: © Brand X Pictures

---

**LIBRARY OF CONGRESS CATALOGING-IN-PUBLICATION DATA**

Homosexuality / David M. Haugen and Matthew J. Box, book editors.
  p. cm. — (Social issues firsthand)
  Includes bibliographical references and index.
  ISBN 0-7377-2891-4 (lib. bdg. : alk. paper)
   1. Homosexuality. 2. Gays—Social conditions. 3. Gays—Identity. 4. Gays—Family relationships. 5. Coming out (Sexual orientation). 6. Homophobia.
  I. Haugen, David M., 1969– . Box, Matthew J., 1976– . III. Series.
  HQ76.25.H6738  2006
  306.76'6—dc22                                                                  2005040258

---

Printed in the United States of America

# CONTENTS

Foreword 7

Introduction: Coming Out: The Process and the Narrative 9

## CHAPTER 1: COMING OUT

**1. The Process of Coming Out** 16
by Jase Wells
A young man speaks of how he first had to admit his homosexuality to himself before he could "come out" to his family and friends.

**2. A Politician Overcomes His Fear of Exposure** 20
by Barney Frank
A U.S. congressman tells of how he feared that making his homosexuality public might negatively impact his career.

**3. A Bisexual Son's Letter to His Mom** 30
by Daniel Peabody
After telling his mother that he is bisexual, a Canadian man writes a letter to her to explain things that were previously left unsaid.

## CHAPTER 2: REACTIONS OF FAMILY MEMBERS

**1. The Father of a Gay Son Is Forced to Address His Own Prejudices** 35
by Jack
After learning that his son is gay, a father confronts his own negative attitudes about homosexuality and begins to question why he has them.

**2. A Mother Feels Guilt over Her Daughter's Homosexuality** 40
by Anonymous
A mother relates her lingering feelings of bitterness and

personal failure after her daughter admits to being a lesbian.

### 3. A Wife Struggles with the Revelation That Her Husband Is Gay  42
by Carol Grever

After a thirty-year marriage, a wife discovers that her husband is gay and must then learn to cope with an uncertain future.

## CHAPTER 3: SELF-ACCEPTANCE AND IDENTITY

### 1. Accepting My Body and Myself  50
by Anna Mills

A lesbian's eating disorders were just one facet of her coming to terms with her body and her closeted homosexuality.

### 2. The Choice of a Gay Identity  54
by Jordan Roth

A theatrical producer argues that while homosexuality is something that one is born with, embracing an openly gay lifestyle is a choice.

### 3. Diary of a Gay Priest  59
by Bruce J. Simpson

An archbishop discusses how his homosexuality compelled him to quit the Catholic seminary but ultimately led him to become an ordained priest in a more tolerant sect of the church.

### 4. A Transsexual Struggles for a True Identity  67
by Alison Lade

A transgender male-to-female speaks of his own acceptance and other people's problems with his identity.

### 5. Living with HIV: A Battle to Stay Alive  75
by David Morris

An HIV survivor asserts that his resolve not to die, coupled with a never-ending series of drug trials and other medical treatments, has helped him stave off the worst disease to ravage the gay community.

## CHAPTER 4: DISCRIMINATION

### 1. Negative Attitudes Toward Homosexuality Have Not Changed
80

by Youth Panel Participants

A gay youth panel argues that the growing number of openly gay characters in popular culture and media is not an indication that mainstream America has become less homophobic.

### 2. Black and Gay: Facing Racism and Homophobia
85

by Ed Brock

A secondary school teacher discusses facing discrimination for being both black and gay.

### 3. A Marine Officer Under "Don't Ask, Don't Tell"
94

by Luke, interviewed by Steven Zeeland

A marine tells of how his pride in being gay is constantly challenged under the policies of the U.S. military.

### 4. Fired for Being Gay
98

by Alice Pedreira, interviewed by Mubarak S. Dahir

A social worker relates the story of how she was fired from her job for being gay—even though she had told her managers that she was a lesbian when she was hired.

## CHAPTER 5: MARRIAGE AND PARENTING

### 1. Tying the Knot in San Francisco
104

by Julie and Danielle, with Steve Zimmerman

Two lesbian partners revel in the fact that after eight years of being denied a marriage license, they were legally wed when San Francisco briefly sanctioned same-sex marriages.

### 2. Lesbian Moms and Their Baby Boy
108

by Jay and Alex

Two Irish lesbians speak of how artificial insemination

allowed them to conceive a son, who has since been a blessing in their lives.

## 3. Why We Chose to Adopt a Child 113
by Dan Savage

A well-known gay columnist writes of how he and his partner had to examine their own motives for wanting to adopt a child.

Organizations to Contact 118
For Further Research 123
Index 126

# FOREWORD

Social issues are often viewed in abstract terms. Pressing challenges such as poverty, homelessness, and addiction are viewed as problems to be defined and solved. Politicians, social scientists, and other experts engage in debates about the extent of the problems, their causes, and how best to remedy them. Often overlooked in these discussions is the human dimension of the issue. Behind every policy debate over poverty, homelessness, and substance abuse, for example, are real people struggling to make ends meet, to survive life on the streets, and to overcome addiction to drugs and alcohol. Their stories are ubiquitous and compelling. They are the stories of everyday people—perhaps your own family members or friends—and yet they rarely influence the debates taking place in state capitols, the national Congress, or the courts.

The disparity between the public debate and private experience of social issues is well illustrated by looking at the topic of poverty. Each year the U.S. Census Bureau establishes a poverty threshold. A household with an income below the threshold is defined as poor, while a household with an income above the threshold is considered able to live on a basic subsistence level. For example, in 2003 a family of two was considered poor if its income was less than $12,015; a family of four was defined as poor if its income was less than $18,810. Based on this system, the bureau estimates that 35.9 million Americans (12.5 percent of the population) lived below the poverty line in 2003, including 12.9 million children below the age of eighteen.

Commentators disagree about what these statistics mean. Social activists insist that the huge number of officially poor Americans translates into human suffering. Even many families that have incomes above the threshold, they maintain, are likely to be struggling to get by. Other commentators insist that the statistics exaggerate the problem of poverty in the United States. Compared to people in developing countries, they point out, most so-called poor families have a high quality of life. As stated by journalist Fidelis Iyebote, "Cars are owned by 70 percent of 'poor' households.... Color televisions belong to 97 percent of the 'poor' [and] videocassette recorders belong to nearly 75 percent.... Sixty-four percent have microwave ovens, half own a stereo system, and over a quarter possess an automatic dishwasher."

However, this debate over the poverty threshold and what it means is likely irrelevant to a person living in poverty. Simply put, poor people do not need the government to tell them whether they are poor. They can see it in the stack of bills they cannot pay. They are aware of it when they are forced to choose between paying rent or buying food for their children. They become painfully conscious of it when they lose their homes and are forced to live in their cars or on the streets. Indeed, the written stories of poor people define the meaning of poverty more vividly than a government bureaucracy could ever hope to. Narratives composed by the poor describe losing jobs due to injury or mental illness, depict horrific tales of childhood abuse and spousal violence, recount the loss of friends and family members. They evoke the slipping away of social supports and government assistance, the descent into substance abuse and addiction, the harsh realities of life on the streets. These are the perspectives on poverty that are too often omitted from discussions over the extent of the problem and how to solve it.

Greenhaven Press's Social Issues Firsthand series provides a forum for the often-overlooked human perspectives on society's most divisive topics of debate. Each volume focuses on one social issue and presents a collection of ten to sixteen narratives by those who have had personal involvement with the topic. Extra care has been taken to include a diverse range of perspectives. For example, in the volume on adoption, readers will find the stories of birth parents who have given up their children for adoption, adoptive parents, and adoptees themselves. After exposure to these varied points of view, the reader will have a clearer understanding that adoption is an intense, emotional experience full of joyous highs and painful lows for all concerned.

Each book in the series contains several features that enhance its usefulness, including an in-depth introduction, an annotated table of contents, bibliographies for further research, a list of organizations to contact, and a thorough index. These elements—combined with the poignant voices of people touched by tragedy and triumph—make the Social Issues Firsthand series a valuable resource for research on today's topics of political discussion.

# INTRODUCTION

# Coming Out: The Process and the Narrative

Many homosexuals keep their sexual identity secret. Therefore, when they decide to make their sexual preference for members of the same sex public, it is known as "coming out of the closet." Coming out is a significant event in the lives of gay men and lesbians. Declaring one's homosexuality in a predominantly heterosexual society is to single oneself out, to distinguish oneself from what is considered normal. The result can be ostracism and harassment as well as praise for being courageous enough to stand up to any negative social judgments. Thus, deciding how, where, and when to come out of the closet is a choice that requires a great deal of consideration.

When deliberating whether to come out, a gay or lesbian person must weigh the potentially negative consequences against the positive benefits of taking such a step. Homosexuals are most likely to come out initially to family and friends—those people who are most trusted and relied upon for emotional support. Even from these typically sympathetic individuals, however, gays and lesbians can expect a range of responses when they make their sexuality known. Some loved ones may react with acceptance or indifference, while others may be shocked and express scorn or hostility. Regardless of their reactions, family members and friends will perceive the newly out gay or lesbian person in a new way, potentially adding stress to even the most accepting relationship.

Widening this audience circle and maintaining an openly homosexual identity in public invites even greater scrutiny. Because it involves embracing an unconventional lifestyle, coming out is a political as well as individual act. Many gays and lesbians resent that being true to their own identity has this political dimension, since the lives of heterosexual people are not similarly burdened.

The relationships any person shares with loved ones are characterized by a high degree of closeness and intimacy. Gays and lesbians face the possibility of disrupting the harmony of such relationships upon revealing their homosexuality. In a book called *Coming Out Right*, authors Wes Muchmore and William Hanson caution homosexuals who are contemplating coming out: "Be prepared for some surprises. The friend you've regarded as the most liberal may turn out to be the one who can't handle the idea that you're gay. Others may accept it intellectually but will become uneasy when confronted by tangible evidence of your sex life, such as your lover."[1] The prospect of losing the love and respect of family members is even more intimidating. While not advocating that gays and lesbians leave their sexuality undisclosed to their parents, Muchmore and Hanson suggest that homosexuals examine their own motives carefully when deciding to come out to family, since the possibility of rejection can have serious consequences.

Besides suffering from the possibly negative opinions of family members, homosexuals will invariably endure the scrutiny of society and the judgment of strangers. Going against the social grain may lessen a person's chances of having a comfortable, happy existence. In other words, to be openly gay in a society in which heterosexuality is the norm is to invite criticism merely because one is outside the conventional norm. A homosexual is likely to be thought of as a gay man or a lesbian instead of just a man or a woman, and this label can affect social contacts with all types of people, from members of the clergy to shopkeepers. In some instances, homophobia might be manifested in subtle ways that simply make heterosexual-homosexual relationships uncomfortable. Some people oppose homosexuality on moral grounds, which can add further tensions to gay-straight relations. At its most extreme, opposition to homosexuality can lead to harassment and even violence. The threat of violence can deter many gays and lesbians from coming out and openly facing such hatred.

In addition to facing these fears, gays must recognize that coming out is not a single, isolated event, but a lifelong process. Unless a person lives in the public eye and his or her lifestyle is highly visible, coming out must take place several times to several people. Anytime a gay man or lesbian changes surroundings or meets someone new, he or she returns to the starting point of the coming-out process. Opening up to a single person or a small group requires less resilience than doing so over and over again for many years. Many gay people feel that they lack the fortitude to come out continually, so they simply shy away from the prospect.

INTRODUCTION

## POSITIVE MOTIVATION FOR COMING OUT

Despite the possibly negative consequences of coming out, there are benefits for those who choose to take that step. For some gays and lesbians, the positives outweigh or neutralize the fears. Moreover, some find the strength to combat negative social attitudes toward homosexuality more effectively once they openly embrace their identity.

Keeping one's true identity hidden is burdensome and exhausting. As author Mary V. Borhek writes, "You have to watch carefully everything you say so you do not let slip some piece of information that might give away your secret."[2] As a result, closeted gays and lesbians often feel as if they are living a lie. This dual life is in part forced upon them by the heterosexual world, but some gays and lesbians also condemn themselves for cooperating in this facade. Maintaining a secret identity can be psychologically harmful for homosexuals. Authors Wes Muchmore and William Hanson state that "life in the closet, with its repressions and falsifications, can create great strains on one's mental health. . . . Self-hatred is extremely difficult to avoid; indeed, choosing total secrecy is in itself a harsh affront to one's true nature."[3] Coming out eases some of this burden by shedding the need to constantly police oneself against saying or doing the wrong thing. It also can give gays and lesbians a sense of unity and the strength to live their lives as they wish. This feeling of liberty and buoyancy is often sufficient motivation for coming out.

Gaining personal liberty is only one reason that many gays and lesbians are motivated to come out. Another factor is acceptance into the community of those who have already taken that step and declared themselves openly gay. Thus, the visibility and collective strength embodied by the gay community provide a healthy, encouraging atmosphere for newcomers. Joining that community gives gay and lesbian individuals the opportunity to take pride in their identity and to work toward social change so the act of coming out will not be such a harrowing experience for future generations of homosexuals.

## A PERSONAL CHOICE

Given the fears and positive motivations, how, when, and if to come out are difficult decisions weighing on the minds of many closeted gays and lesbians. Ultimately, coming out is a personal choice carried out at the discretion of the gay individual, and the event often happens at a critical stage in life when that person is ready to accept his or her identity. Gary Dowd says in his coming-out story that "the most important thing for me about coming out was knowing that I was ready to do it. Before I came out to anyone, I wanted to feel one hundred percent comfortable and content with my gayness, and experienced enough to know what I was talking about."[4] Deciding that personal comfort is more important than the perceptions of others is a form of psychological awakening, and many gay and lesbian people are motivated to come out as a means of acquiring self-confidence and personal strength. Mathematical psychologist Gregory M. Griffin writes in the afterword to *Beyond Acceptance: Parents of Lesbians and Gays Talk About Their Experiences* that "being gay . . . offers an uncommonly powerful catalyst for personal transformation. If we can stand the heat and give ourselves over to the full scope of the process of coming out, we will learn flexibility in the midst of life's chaos, paradox, and mystery."[5] Thus, the act of coming out not only restores order to emotionally burdened lives, but also provides people with the ability to navigate future problems with confidence. While the process itself carries its own set of successes and failures, those who choose to initiate it are, in Griffin's view, moving toward a better quality of life.

## WRITING THE COMING-OUT STORY

Many people who have chosen to come out of the closet gain a sense of personal liberation and wish to share this feeling with others. Many gays and lesbians, for example, write about their decision to come out. Writing a coming-out narrative is a way for gay men and women to explain, define, and celebrate their identity. At the same time, the coming-out story allows gays and lesbians to reveal themselves to a wider audience, since, once written and published (whether in a book or journal or on a Web site), the narrative becomes a testimony open to public inspection.

Many gays and lesbians write about their coming-out experiences in order to reveal how significant and rewarding the act can be. Some authors make explicit the negative perceptions they had prior to coming out and, as a result, construct their stories to show how unfounded some of those fears were. By eliminating misconceptions, coming-out stories can give encouragement to those who are contemplating whether to come out themselves.

## INTRODUCTION

Offering encouragement is only one aspect of the coming-out story, though. As gay author and activist John Preston notes, coming-out stories and other narratives about being gay were important to him in his formative years because they were about "my place in the world."[6] Thus, stories written by homosexuals show not only how they contend with the ups and downs of being gay in a heterosexual world, but ultimately how they have found a place in that world. As Preston asserts, these stories have a power over gay and lesbian readers—"a power that gives hope and destroys isolation."[7]

The gay narrative can also be as simple as a tribute to the experience of being gay itself. Some authors just desire to celebrate the accomplishment of finally reconciling and accepting their identity. Their story serves no other purpose than to give form to an experience that was unique to them, like a religious epiphany. As twenty-four-year-old Rick Cary says of his coming-out story, "[It] has not ended, because I am continually coming out. I will always need to reaffirm the goodness of my gayness and share that pearl with people I care about."[8] Cary's story is for him a signpost that points to the moment in time when he truly became himself.

Finally, since the coming-out story can reach a heterosexual as well as a homosexual audience, it can serve a socially instructive purpose. Writing about being gay or lesbian is one way in which homosexuals add to society's awareness about gay lifestyles and values. Such narratives can force readers to reconcile these values with the values of society at large. Thus, the coming-out narrative—like the act of coming out itself—not only tells an individual's story, but also tells society about itself. It can test readers' tolerance for lifestyle choices and personal experiences that are unfamiliar, and at the same time it can show that many of the emotional conflicts faced by homosexuals, as well as the power to overcome these struggles are common to people from all walks of life.

## NOTES

1. Wes Muchmore and William Hanson, *Coming Out Right: A Handbook for the Gay Male*. Boston: Alyson, 1991, p. 19.
2. Mary V. Borhek, *Coming Out to Parents: A Two-Way Survival Guide for Lesbians and Gay Men and Their Parents*. Cleveland: Pilgrim Press, 1993, p. 21.
3. Muchmore and Hanson, *Coming Out Right*, p. 22.

4. Gary Dowd, in Ann Heron, ed., *Two Teenagers in Twenty: Writings by Gay and Lesbian Youth*. Boston: Alyson, 1994, p. 45.
5. Gregory M. Griffin, Afterword, in Carolyn Welch Griffin, Marian J. Wirth, and Arthur G. Wirth, *Beyond Acceptance: Parents of Lesbians and Gays Talk About Their Experiences*. New York: St. Martin's, 1996, p. 222.
6. John Preston, "The Importance of Telling Our Stories," in Betty Berzon, ed., *Positively Gay: New Approaches to Gay and Lesbian Life*. Berkeley, CA: Celestial Arts, 1992, p. 23.
7. Preston, "The Importance of Telling Our Stories," p. 25.
8. Rick Cary, in Ann Heron, ed., *Two Teenagers in Twenty: Writings by Gay and Lesbian Youth*. Boston: Alyson, 1994, p. 109.

# CHAPTER 1

## Coming Out

SOCIAL ISSUES FIRSTHAND

# The Process of Coming Out

by Jase Wells

Jase Wells is a thirty-two-year-old information technology specialist living in San Francisco. He "came out," or became openly gay, in February 1993 and since then has had a positive experience living as a gay man. He now lives happily with his partner, Michael.

In the following article, Wells relates the story of his coming out. Wells says that the signs of his sexuality were evident from an early age, but he denied them in order to conform to the status quo in the small town of West Fargo, North Dakota, where he grew up. He also explains that he even attempted to "go steady" with girls during his high school years even though he was aware that he was attracted to men.

While in college at Moorhead University in Minnesota, Wells further developed his sexuality by creating a gay identity online and entering gay chat rooms. While he was exploring his sexuality during this period, he was still in denial about his orientation. When his scholarship ended, he made the choice to move to California at the end of his freshman year in 1992 to be with his mother.

Wells states that the moment he knew for certain that he was gay was when he made arrangements to fly to South Dakota to meet up with a girl he had met online. There was no physical attraction between them, and Wells knew then that he "simply wasn't meant to be heterosexual." After this event, Wells decided to come out. He first came out to his mother, whose response was positive. Subsequently, Wells came out to the rest of his family and friends to mixed degrees of surprise and support.

Although he is "visibly out" with his partner and is not afraid to tell people the truth when they ask him about his sexuality, Wells still describes his coming out as an ongoing process.

Jase Wells, "Coming Out," www.jasewells.com, 2004. Copyright © 2004 by Jason Wells. All rights reserved. Reproduced by permission.

# COMING OUT

I suppose in retrospect, I should have always known I'm gay. If I look hard enough, I can recognize some of the signs in high school, grade school, and even my early childhood. But regardless, I denied any feelings and questions about my sexuality and repressed them, because I had the impression that those kinds of thoughts were wrong. That impression didn't come from my family, though—they never made any direct remarks about homosexuality one way or the other. But as a boy growing up in North Dakota, there were always plenty of subtle cues that society didn't care much for queers. Homosexuals were often the targets of many adolescent jokes.

As much as I tried to deny it, I knew that I was attracted—physically and emotionally—to persons of my own sex. So while the other guys in high school drooled over the swimsuit issue of *Sports Illustrated*, I checked out the well-dressed men of *GQ* and the hunky bodies in *Men's Fitness*. And when I finally turned 18, I was like a kid in a candy shop at the local adult bookstore—it was the first time I'd ever seen *Mandate* or other male porn magazines. The first few times I'd always buy a "straight" magazine along with a few gay ones. The lady would look at me funny, then give me my purchase in a plain brown paper bag. Within a few months I finally found the courage to forget about the extra straight magazine, and I didn't get any more funny looks.

## DENIAL AT SCHOOL

Throughout high school and my first year of college, I was completely in the closet without even admitting that there was a closet to be in. I even "went steady" with two girls at different times during high school. And in both cases, as the girl started getting more serious about me, something clicked and I had to get out of the relationship. I knew I didn't want to be physical with the opposite sex. My hormones told me I wanted to be physical with the same sex, and I found ways to do so. But after fooling around, I'd always feel terribly ashamed and empty. I always promised myself to never do it again, but my hormones never cared much about those promises.

After high school I enrolled in nearby Moorhead State University, mostly because they offered me a full scholarship and it was hard to justify turning it down. My Freshman year there was rather uneventful, but thanks to my Computer Science classes I discovered some online chat rooms . . . where I developed an online identity to explore what it might be like to be gay. I also heard about the Ten Percent Society on campus, and I wanted to go—as a supportive "straight" person—but I never had enough courage to do so. After my Freshman year, my scholarship ended (at least that's what I told everyone; technically I could have renewed it) and my mom invited me to live with her in California. I had been wanting to move to the Golden State for so long, and it was finally my chance to do it! In the fall of 1992, I packed everything I had into my little car and drove across the country. . . .

But even after I moved to California, I was still confused and in denial about my sexuality. I saw how gay people are ostracized and ridiculed, and I didn't want to be gay. Part of me thought that if I could be with a woman, then everything would fall into place and I'd be over my attraction to men. So in one of the more foolish and irresponsible events of my life, I flew to South Dakota to meet a girl with whom I'd become close friends via an online chat forum. To make a long story short, we did end up having sex, and I realized that I simply wasn't meant to be heterosexual. The emotional love and physical excitement just wasn't there. The experience certainly made everything fall into place, but just not like I had thought it would.

## COMING OUT TO MYSELF, MY FAMILY, AND MY FRIENDS

So, I finally knew that I'm gay. On February 23, 1993, I came out to myself. (I remember the date because it happened to be, strangely enough, my father's birthday!) I also came out to my mom that day, with whom I was still living at the time. I was so nervous, but I knew it was something I had to do. I was shaking, but somehow after plenty of stumbling and stuttering I said the big G word. And to my surprise—and delight—my mom let out a deep breath and said something like "Is that all?". She thought I was going to say that I didn't like California and wanted to move back to North Dakota. She hugged me and told me it didn't matter if I'm gay. As it turns out, I later found out that my mom's best friend from high school is gay, too. So it certainly wasn't an issue with her.

The next task was to tell my family and friends back in North Dakota. After such a positive experience with my mom, I couldn't wait to tell everyone. My younger sister was surprised, but still supportive. My dad admitted that he wasn't ecstatic about the news, but he made it a point to tell me he still loved me just the same. Some of my friends were shocked; some said they had guessed it already.

All in all, it was a pretty good coming out—whether they were surprised or not, everyone was supportive and positive.

By now, it's simply a matter of fact to my family and friends that I'm gay. I never have to remind anyone about my sexuality or what Michael means in my life. Ironically, I do have to remind them that my name isn't Jason anymore! (By coincidence, I adopted my nickname Jase as my real name at the same time I came out.) All three of my parents are completely accepting of the relationship between Michael and me, and we all get along wonderfully.

## COMING OUT IS A CONTINUAL PROCESS

Still, coming out is a continual process. Just by wearing gold bands on our ring fingers, Michael and I are making a decision to be visibly out. If somebody asks me about it, I'll tell them the truth—that I have a husband, not a wife. When I interviewed for my post-college employment, I had to decide whether or not I would be visibly out by including in my web portfolio the sites I've done that have gay content. It was really an easy decision for me, though, as I certainly wouldn't want to work anywhere that had a problem with my sexuality. And I knew that I'd be hired based on my talents, not based on the sex of who I love.

# A Politician Overcomes His Fear of Exposure

by Barney Frank

The arena of politics poses a special challenge for those who decide to publicly reveal their sexuality. In most cases, political success depends on having an image that a majority of voters are comfortable aligning with, and admitted homosexuality could put off both constituents and political allies.

A case in point is Massachusetts congressman Barney Frank. Frank personally acknowledged his sexuality once he hit his teenage years, but, as he explains in the following narrative, he made the choice to keep it a secret for two more decades. As his profession became a more significant aspect of his life, he viewed coming out as a threat to his livelihood as a politician.

Frank was afraid that his homosexuality would detract from voter support and lessen his credibility with other members of Congress if he made it public. He attempted to gauge the reaction of several of his friends and colleagues, but they merely reaffirmed his own fears. As a consolation for not actually coming out, Frank explains that he attempted to do the next best thing: create and support legislation that would ease the burden of living an alternative lifestyle in Massachusetts.

Frank eventually made the decision to come out in 1987. He admits that his previous fears were unfounded because he received no backlash from his colleagues, the press, or the voters. His public life continued as before, and his private life was actually enhanced once the burden of secrecy was removed.

In the spring of 1987, I decided to acknowledge, publicly and voluntarily, that I am gay. Once I definitely decided that I should come out, I had to deal with the question of how. As a member of the U.S. House of Representatives, I recognized that my sexuality would be a matter of some public interest, with a potentially significant impact on my own political career and, to a lesser degree, on public discus-

Barney Frank, "Yeah. So What?" *Out in the Workplace: The Pleasures and Perils of Coming Out on the Job,* edited by Richard A. Rasi and Lourdes Rodríguez-Nogués. Los Angeles: Alyson Publications, 1995. Copyright © 1995 by Barney Frank. Reproduced by permission.

sion of homosexuality. I sounded out several people whose judgment I respected, reflected on what I'd learned in four years of college, five years in a Ph.D. program, and three years of law school, thought about the lessons of twenty years of active political work, and drew heavily on my lifelong study of political rhetoric to conclude that what I wanted was for a reporter to ask me if I were gay and for me to answer, "Yeah. So what?" That is what happened—in part. Kay Longcope of *The Boston Globe* asked, and I responded with that answer.

From the perspective of 1995, several elements of this strategy now seem unduly defensive. I had expected the results to be a trade-off in which enormous gains in my personal life would outweigh setbacks in my standing with the voters and my ability to influence congressional colleagues. Happily, I was wrong. Not only were the gains in my personal life much greater than I would have predicted—meeting my lover, Herb Moses, being the most profound—but the negative effect on the political side was close to nonexistent.

I can say in defense of my having miscalculated so much on the pessimistic side that I did not make this mistake alone. A large number of friends with whom I discussed my coming out urged me not to do so, predicting political consequences ranging from mildly discomforting all the way to dire. While their counsel did not ultimately dissuade me, it did lead me to be much more careful about coming out than I have been about anything else I have ever done.

## STAYING IN THE CLOSET

I realized that I was gay when I was thirteen: that is, I recognized a fact over which I had absolutely no control and about which I was decidedly unhappy. (I find it hard to believe that anyone would really think that a thirteen-year-old kid living in New Jersey in 1953 would have decided that spending the rest of his life as a homosexual was a really neat idea.) For the next twenty years, I lived in terror that anybody else would find out, and I had little occasion to meet other gay people in normal social or professional settings.

In May 1972, I decided to run for a Massachusetts State House seat that was being vacated in the Beacon Hill and Back Bay sections of Boston. This opportunity required me to decide how to deal with being gay. Coming out was unthinkable—and not simply because it would have meant I couldn't win. The notion of going from being completely closeted to being one of America's most public homosexuals—the consequence of running as a gay legislative candidate in 1972—was far beyond my emotional capacity. At the same time, I was by then already angry at the world and at myself because I was suppressing so vital a part of my personality. I decided that I would run and that I would stay closeted but that I would be a strong, unyielding supporter of gay rights. I would vindicate through my public work what I so fiercely kept hidden in my private life.

## WORKING FOR GAY RIGHTS

I did not think there were many gay men and lesbians living in my future district, partly because there were fewer than now live there, but even more because despite the nascent gay rights political movement then present in Boston, most of us were still keeping our closet doors tightly shut. Thus I was not pressured into taking an aggressive pro-gay and pro-lesbian position; the generally sophisticated attitudes prevalent in those neighborhoods, however, produced a range of reactions to my gay rights advocacy from tolerance to admiration. I worked with new gay and lesbian friends on various issues. For example, after the election I filed two gay rights bills. One would have repealed the law against private consensual sex between adults, and another would have banned any discrimination against people based on their sexual preference. Neither bill went very far legislatively, but they did begin the public discussion of gay rights in Massachusetts.

The antidiscrimination bill I had filed was the first to be given a hearing. I clearly remember how nervous I was. This was the first time in my life I would be discussing gay rights in a forum composed primarily of straight people, most of whom I assumed would be either indifferent or hostile. I was at the time an unmarried thirty-three-year-old man, appearing in public as the first legislator in Massachusetts history to offer and push for a bill to end discrimination against gay people. I worried that I would be asked if I were gay, and I was so unsettled by the possibility that I couldn't even calmly think of a good way to respond. I also worried about the possibility that many people would read or hear about my work on the bill and simply assume I was gay. And short of paying a woman to interrupt my testimony by serving me with papers for a paternity suit, I couldn't think of anything I could do to counter that assumption.

It turned out that the consensual sex bill, which would have repealed the sodomy law, created the bigger stir. It was defeated by a vote of approximately 210 to 11. But before voting it down, dozens of legislators pushed the "yes" switch on their desks, temporarily giving the bill an overwhelming majority on the board. They then uproariously switched to "no." I was not offended, but the next day Carol Liston of *The Boston Globe* wrote an eloquent, blistering attack on my colleagues for not simply killing the bill, but instead making a joke out of something so important to so many citizens. The column rang true, and several colleagues apologized to me after reading it. It was the *Globe*'s lead op-ed piece for that day, an important mark of respect for our cause from mainstream society.

The concrete result of all this was nothing much, but for me it was a very important nothing. No matter what various people may have thought, nobody asked, said, or did anything about my sexuality. Consequently, I felt confirmed in my view that I could maintain a bifurcated existence—remaining totally closeted while playing an active public role as a leader in the gay rights fight.

And I did, for the next seven years, despite an event that, logically, should have persuaded me that I could come out and still remain in the legislature. In 1974, Elaine Noble ran for a new seat in the House. The seat had been created after redistricting and was made up to a great degree of areas that had been in my district when I won in 1972. Elaine was open about her lesbianism. While this was an issue used against her, she defeated a credible neighborhood activist in the primary and a well-financed independent candidate in November.

Why did this event have so little impact on my opening the door of the closet? After all, Noble's victory undermined my stated reason for being so resolutely secretive about my homosexuality: namely, to preserve the option of a political career. At that point, I still considered myself lucky to have won a State House seat in my unusually cosmopolitan, sophisticated district. As a Jewish, closeted gay man from New Jersey who spoke with a noticeable non-Massachusetts accent and was fifty pounds overweight, I thought I was much too unconventional a candidate to ever win a larger constituency. My long-standing insecurity about being gay and an attendant fear of rejection led me to rationalize, however, that while Elaine could pull it off, I could not. I continued to be as active in the fight against homophobia as any politician in America, but I continued to convince myself that coming out would jeopardize my career.

## RECONSIDERING THE ACT OF GOING PUBLIC

By 1979, events were again converging to make me think about publicly acknowledging my gayness. First and most powerfully, I was increasingly realizing—and regretting—the harm I was doing myself by trying to suppress all evidence of so important a part of me. I was more and more jealous of my gay and lesbian friends with whom I was socializing, whose social and physical intimacies I envied. And while I did not realize it very clearly yet, this unhappiness with my life was having a negative effect on the way I was doing my job. While being totally closeted had probably helped advance my career at first, since it meant I had few social distractions to take me away from work, the corrosive effect this way of living had on my self-esteem and my emotional balance by now definitely detracted from my work.

Another reason I wanted more and more to acknowledge my gayness publicly was that I now knew many other homosexuals and saw how they could live strong, healthy, normal lives. The notion of telling other people that I was gay no longer seemed such a terrible leap. In fact, while I was still paradoxically convinced that, unlike Elaine Noble, I could not come out of the closet and stay in the House, that no longer seemed to me such a bad deal.

So I started to come out.

For me, approaching the age of forty in late 1979, the only possible way to do this was to come out to one close friend or relative at a time, with intervals of a few weeks to recharge my emotional batteries sufficiently to empower the next confession—since, alas, that is what it still felt like to me. Everyone took it very well, with the gay people I told expressing a great deal less surprise than the straight ones.

I had barely reached double numbers when politics and the pope intervened dramatically. Pope John Paul II ordered Father Robert Drinan from the adjoining district not to run for reelection to the U.S. Congress. My subsequent decision to run for Drinan's seat required a number of choices, but one option no longer seemed open—acknowledging my sexuality. In fact, I told my sister and brother-in-law, Doris and Jim Breay, about my running for Congress in a phone call that I began by saying, "You are about to hear a closet door slamming shut." I was very worried about the possibility that I would be "accused" of homosexuality during that campaign, and I still did not know how to respond.

My support of gay rights was used against me in the campaign along with a number of other issues that were tied together with some success to portray me as an alien, valueless big-city type poaching on a suburban and semirural district. I won, but only narrowly, in both the primary and the final election.

When I got to Washington after the November 1980 election, I gave a great deal of thought to how to deal with being gay. I was not remotely ready to come out publicly, but neither was I prepared to re-create the hermetically sealed private life from which I had just begun to emerge.

## LIVING A DUAL LIFE

My initial response to this dilemma is very relevant to contemporary discussions about how we gay men and lesbians should live our lives, because I tried hard for the next six years to live the way many straight people tell us we should live. Their question is essentially "It's okay for you to be gay, but why do you have to make a big deal of it? Can't you just do what you want to without telling everybody?" The position urged on us by this attitude is literally impossible to maintain. No one can get through a week's interaction with other human beings without revealing his or her sexual orientation except by either lying outright or refusing to answer the normal civil questions that make up much casual conversation: "What did you do last weekend?" "Where will you spend the holidays?" "Are you married?" "Do you want to bring a date to the party?"

My most compelling evidence that this is an impossible way to live without a great deal of evasion, double-talk, and outright dishonesty is my attempt to do so from 1981 to mid 1987. It did not work. From the time I arrived in Washington. I was out to other gay men and lesbians but not to the public. In effect, I tried to live a dual life. With straight people, I ignored my sexuality and made no references to it. Privately, I spent much of my time socializing with other gay people, with no effort to hide my identity. This mode of life became more and more difficult. I was uncomfortable once again with dissembling before straight people. The fact that I was a member of Congress, whose comings and goings were of some relevance to the media, exacerbated the problem, since it meant I had less privacy than most other people do.

What I learned was that, once again, Abraham Lincoln was right. I could not spend half my time as a gay man in private while enslaving myself to antigay prejudice the other half of the time. Asking others to share my life at that point means asking them to follow a very peculiar set of rules about when to acknowledge gayness and when implicitly to deny it—or at least avoid it in ways that could lead to awkwardness at best and de facto hypocrisy at worst. As it became increasingly clear to me that this solution was not working either, my emotional state worsened to the point of a stupid involvement with a hustler which was later to cause me significant embarrassment. I became involved with this individual in 1985, at the same time as I was still trying to coexist as half gay and half none of the above.

## PREPARING TO COME OUT

At any rate, by 1986 I was determined to complete the process of coming out. This determination was not motivated, however, by mounting fears of exposure. Neither the closeted gay reporters nor the openly straight ones ever so much as suggested that they would make a public issue of my sexuality until and unless I chose to.

Confirmation that the press would not break the story against my will came in the summer of 1986, when I was outed in the autobiography of former Congressman Robert Bauman, a Republican who had lost his seat in 1980 after himself being outed. The press declined to publicize my outing to any great degree. One magazine printed the excerpt of the book relevant to me, but with my name deleted.

## SOME REACTIONS IN WASHINGTON

This incident did serve, however, as sort of trial coming-out for me. When I learned that some newspapers might publicize Bauman's comments, I thought it best to prepare some of my colleagues for the revelation that might be coming. The most interesting reaction I received came from Tip O'Neill. At first he assured me that no one would accept what Bauman had said. I replied that while I was not volunteering the information, it was, in fact, true. His reaction was troubling, not because of any negative feeling by him, but as a reading of the effect this revelation would have on my general political standing. The thrust of his remarks was that I had damaged my career and that any chance I might have had to be in the House leadership no longer existed.

At first this reply bothered me and caused me to feel a little sorry for myself. I reminded myself that I was already enjoying the great privilege of serving Congress, where I felt free to pursue issues according to what I saw was right, with few political constraints, and that I had tried every possible variant of dealing with being gay short of simple candor—without finding a satisfactory alternative. To start backsliding because it might hinder an already extremely slender chance to join the House leadership was not sensible. I thus felt free to resume my slow march toward "outness."

By the summer of 1986, the fact that I was gay and might be planning to talk about it was not one of Washington's better-kept secrets. Some of my straight, liberal House colleagues discussed this with me, and, overwhelmingly, their view was that I should not make any public statement. To do so, they said, would be to risk "marginalizing" myself. My views on every other issue would be discounted, and I would be recast as a single-issue congressman. Their arguments were flattering—couched in terms of not wanting to lose my advocacy for other major issues—but also, of course, a little depressing.

All of us at that point assumed that I would pay some price in diminished influence on some issues for being candid about my sexuality. Unlike my gay and lesbian friends, straight people tended to see little reason to pay that price. Generally, they underestimated the importance to me personally of dropping all pretense and equally underestimated the public importance of my making a simple statement that I am gay.

The very fact that so many decent, wholly well-intentioned political leaders—themselves strong and effective opponents of homophobia—understood so little why coming out was important made it even more clear to me just how important it really was. Even my closest political allies saw the semicloset in which I was living as a perfectly reasonable way to deal with prejudice. They urged me to continue living a life that was costing me a great deal emotionally, thus demonstrating to me that we would not be successful in abolishing homophobia without doing a better job of telling the straight majority exactly what it is all about.

Thus paradoxically but profoundly, the advice I got not to come out strengthened my resolve to do so. But it simultaneously strengthened my conviction that this was something to be approached very carefully, so that I could do it in a way that minimized the political damage almost everyone foresaw. My solution was to accelerate a process I came to think of as "leaking out." By the mid 1980s enough people had figured out that I was gay that I could joke about it with both straight and gay friends. I was even enjoying the fact that I could finally make light of being gay, after years of schlepping it around as if it were the world's heaviest burden. This in itself was a very important sign to me that self-hatred was rapidly disappearing from my psychological makeup. Directing humor at myself had, I believe, a disarming quality and made it less likely that my gayness would be used as a weapon against me.

## THE CONSEQUENCES OF GOING PUBLIC

As it turned out, when I did finally give Kay Longcope the answer I had told her she could elicit, and *The Boston Globe* printed it on June 1, 1987, the consequences were far better than I had anticipated. Politically, it had no negative effect either on my ability to win reelection to the House or on my ability to function within that institution.

I have run for reelection three times since coming out. An estimate from a 1987 poll that I might lose about two or three percentage points turned out to be accurate, but even so I was reelected in 1988 by a margin of 70 percent to 30 percent. Two years later, I won 66 percent to 34 percent in what was generally a bad year for Democratic congressional candidates. In 1992, I received 68 percent of the vote as compared to 26 percent for the Republican candidate and 5 percent for the Ross Perot candidate. In 1994, I ran unopposed.

Also subsequent to my announcement I was asked by the House leadership to run for the Budget Committee, and I was appointed in 1993 to the speaker's leadership advisory group. The two most respected evaluators of congressional reputation, the *Almanac of American Politics*, published by the *National Journal*, and *Politics of America*, published by *Congressional Quarterly*, explicitly asserted that coming out did no damage whatsoever to my standing in the House. In fact, being out has clearly enhanced my effectiveness as a member of Congress, precisely because it has benefited me so much personally.

Since November 1994 I have been working with the Democratic House leadership in its opposition to the conservative Republican House majority. Early efforts by the Republicans to delegitimize me by stressing my sexual orientation backfired, and I do not believe many people think that my being gay in any way detracts from my participation in the leadership effort.

The personal consequences of my public coming-out have been extraordinarily favorable. The most important of these was meeting my lover, Herb Moses, in August 1987. He has transformed my personal life and is the major reason, I think, that I am in a frame of mind to do my job more effectively. My relationship with Herb has since led to a second coming-out, this time as one half of a gay couple.

Herb and I decided early on that we would do things as a couple just as other couples do them. We do these things not to make a statement but simply because they are the kinds of things couples naturally want to do together. The fact that we are together in a wide variety of environments and circumstances in which gay or lesbian couples have not previously been visible helps the fight against homophobia.

In the end, any assessment of my coming-out decision ultimately boils down to a good news/bad news analysis.

The good news is that coming out brought none of the negative consequences I anticipated. But the fact that I did find myself anticipating them is bad news and the very fact that I had to come out at all, even worse. In a rational and unprejudiced world, I would have let people know I was gay as soon as I found out, just as I have with every other important aspect of my life, without worrying a great deal about the consequences.

Analogously, regarding homophobia in general the good news is that there is a lot less of it than there used to be, the bad news is that it ever existed in the first place, and the worse news is that it remains far stronger than is healthy for a society dedicated in theory to equality under the law.

Remembering how far we've come toward the goal of equality, as well as how far we have to go to reach it, are both essential if we are to get there.

# A Bisexual Son's Letter to His Mom

by Daniel Peabody

The process of "coming out" to friends and family can be a terrifying ordeal for many homosexuals. Informing one's parents is especially difficult because rejection would rob one of the security and sense of belonging that a family provides. Daniel Peabody, a bisexual man from Ottawa, Canada, faced such tribulation when he confided his sexual orientation to his mother. Although his mother, in Peabody's words, "handled it ok," Peabody felt compelled to follow up his revelation with a letter to his mother that further explained why he no longer wanted to hide his secret from her. In that letter, excerpted below, Peabody reassures his mother that he is happy with his life and that she need not fear the dangers that attend his bisexual lifestyle. Ultimately, Peabody seeks his mother's love and understanding and recognizes that she also may need support in accepting his bisexuality.

Dear Mom,
 It has now been about two weeks since I told you that I am bisexual. You seem to have handled it ok, although I sense you may be feeling hurt and shocked inside by my disclosure. I want to tell you why I chose to come out to you.
 The main reason for telling you is because I no longer want to hide this important part of who I am from you. Because I love you, trust you, and have faith in you, I had to tell you. Mom, I am bisexual, I have always been and always will be. I have always known this; however I used to feel that this was wrong, that I was in someway inferior. I know now that I am not. Ever since I was a small child I knew I was also attracted to males. This doesn't mean that I hate women; this does mean that I am also inclined to fall in love with and share my life with another man. You may feel that my bisexuality is a phase—that it will go away. That's not going to happen, mom. I have struggled to understand myself for nearly two

decades. This was something I had to go through alone and in a very hostile homophobic environment. Your struggle with my lifestyle doesn't need to be alone; you can talk to me, to friends and family, to other parents of lesbian and gay children. You have resources for support—I knew of none and therefore had none.

## ANTICIPATING QUESTIONS

You may be wondering what turned me bi. What went wrong? The simple answer is: Nothing. Nothing turned me bi because I have been bisexual since birth. Nothing went wrong because I am not deviant: I have grown into a self-aware person who is in touch with myself and my desires. I am a good person who, yes, is also attracted to members of the same gender. In the same way that you have never made a decision to be heterosexual, neither have I made a conscious choice to be bisexual. It is something that simply [is] there and I have accepted. Being bi is simply a part of who I am.

Why didn't I discuss this before? For the majority of my life I tried to suppress, change, and hide the fact that I was bi. The thought that I was one of "those people" horrified me. Again: does this mean I hate women? Does this mean I abuse children? Does this mean I'll die from disease? Am I insane? The answer to all these is, of course, NO. I know the homophobic stereotypes; I grew up believing they were true about me and all other bi and gay people. They are false stereotypes, based on fear and hate, not fact. Eventually, I stopped considering myself as a deviant. I am merely different, not less or more equal than any other person on this planet. However, going to high school in [the small town of] Smiths Falls was not the place where I could share this with anyone: I understand what it is like to live in homophobic environments. Then when I transferred to Ottawa: A chance to start over, to leave the rednecks behind, a place where I could find freedom. I did not find it. Living there forced me deeper into my closet. I assumed the trappings of a straight, male teenager. I told homophobic jokes; I got a girlfriend; I met the expectations demanded of my role. I hid my sexuality from you, my family and my friends. I felt I would always lead my double life. However, I am no longer in this situation. I live for me now. With good friends, gay and straight, in my life. They don't have a problem with my bisexuality. They know that this is not a phase; it is an aspect of who I am. They accept me for who I am. I can only hope that one day my whole family will reach this stage of acceptance and understanding.

## NO LONGER A NEED TO HIDE

My sexual orientation doesn't affect the type of person I am, the type of friend I have been or will continue to be. The reason I choose to tell people that I am bi is because I care for and respect them enough not to hide this part of my life from them. I don't do it to hurt, scare or shock them; I do it to express how close I feel to them and to put an end to my need to hide such an important part of my life from them.

I realize you are worried about me. You may be feeling fear that I will face discrimination, diseases, or won't truly be happy. I am optimistic about my life. I realize that there are bigots and fanatics who will hate me simply because of what they assume I do with my penis. These people are misguided and have made decisions based on fear, stereotypes, misinformation and prejudice. I feel sorry for them; it is their loss because they will never get to know me. Homophobes are not people that can bother me because they don't matter in my life. I hope that I won't need to include any family members in this group. I would sorely miss them. I hope for and work towards the day when all people regardless of their differences, feel love towards each other, not hate and fear (if not in my lifetime, maybe the next). On the topic of disease I can only say that I'm bi, not stupid. I take care of myself. I educate myself and I don't put myself at risk or in risky situations. Safer sex is an absolute must, not just for myself but everyone who has sex. The truth is sex can kill you, gay or straight. I work hard to educate myself and others about the risks associated with any sexual activities. And Mom, I am happy and will likely remain so. Letting people know that I am bi removes the need to lead a double life; the need to hide who I am; and the incorrect role expectations placed on me. Coming out has given me the opportunity to seek satisfying longterm relationships instead of closeted relationships which were emotionally unfulfilling.

## SUPPORT

I'm sure that you are feeling more things than I have brought up here. I am probably not the best person to help you through your feelings. I hope you are going to contact PFLAG (Parents and Friends of Lesbians And Gays). I don't mean to push you into accepting me, but I hope it takes you less time than it took me. I don't want to be nearly 40 before I can say my mother loves me and accepts I'm bi. Note that this isn't saying "loves me despite my being" or "because I'm bi." All I need is acceptance, tolerance, and love. I love you; you are the only mother I will ever have. Please understand that I will always need your love and support, and in telling you I am bi I am trying to bring myself closer to you: openly and honestly. I don't want communication to end and our relationship to dry up. Coming out and telling you I am bi is the only way I can truly and honestly share my life with you. Being bi is a part of who I am but not all of who I am. I want to remain, first and foremost, your son and not be reduced to your bi/gay son or the son you never speak to. I want you to be able to ask me anything about myself, and I want you to remain involved in my life. If I were to continue to hide my bisexuality from you, I could not have a real relationship with you; it would be a creation which would not be completely honest, open, and truthful. Please contact PFLAG. Trust me—dealing with this alone takes far too long and is far too painful. These people will not judge you; they will listen, provide support and understanding.

Please remember I will always love you and will always be your son. I also need you to understand that I will always be bi and can not be changed, the same way that a straight person should not, would not, and could not be turned gay nor a gay person straight. Please don't hide the fact that you have a bi child. It is not a reflection on you; it is an expression of who I am. You needn't be embarrassed or ashamed of who I am, because I am: Daniel Peabody-Douwsma, a good person who you can be proud of. If people or God are going to judge me based on who I am, then I am not worried: I know that I am as important and as worthy of love, life, and freedom as anyone else.

My Love Always,
Daniel

# CHAPTER 2

*Reactions of Family Members*

SOCIAL ISSUES FIRSTHAND

# The Father of a Gay Son Is Forced to Address His Own Prejudices

by Jack

> In the following narrative, Jack, a sixty-three-year-old professor at a midwestern university, examines some of his own homophobic attitudes in the wake of learning that one of his sons is a homosexual. Nine years previous to the writing of this story, Jack's son, Chris, told his parents that he was gay, and he arranged for family counseling to help his parents and his two siblings adjust to the revelation. Jack went to the counseling sessions, and he maintains that they helped keep him from initially reacting harshly. However, Jack still had to contend with all the negative stereotypes that informed his inculcated "distaste" for homosexuality. He admitted to Chris that it was difficult news to accept, and that while he was adjusting to his son's gayness, Chris would have to accept his father's unease. Over time, Jack learned that his personal "hang-ups" were jeopardizing his relationship with his son. He also recognized that his inability to be open to his son's identity was just one of many ways in which he was imprisoned by social prejudices and ignorance.

I remember when Chris told us he was gay. We were stunned, and for a time his announcement was followed by silence. Then he started to cry. I just went over and put my arms around him.

I was shaken by it. I had a lot of mixed feelings. Chris was in training as a clinical psychologist, and he had talked with a therapist about the possibility of our coming to see him. The whole family went the next day. That was a big help. We got feelings out. Part of me was kind of numb. I hadn't really accepted it, but having a chance to talk it out was a lucky break. It was a useful thing for that

Carolyn Welch Griffin, Marian J. Wirth, and Arthur G. Wirth, *Beyond Acceptance: Parents of Lesbians and Gays Talk About Their Experiences.* New York: Prentice-Hall, Inc., 1986. Copyright © 1986 by Prentice-Hall, Inc. Reproduced by permission.

immediate occasion, but it didn't get me around the corner in terms of really accepting homosexuality.

Fairly soon we flew back home, and got in touch with the local gay church to find out if there was a parents' group. There wasn't, but we were invited to attend one of their services.

The church service really shook me. I had trouble fighting back the tears during the service. There were gay and lesbian couples going up to the altar together holding hands. I wasn't feeling positive about that. I was thinking, "Is Chris going to be into something like this?" I was feeling sorry for myself that that would happen. But I had all sorts of mixed feelings, because I also thought there were very tender feelings between these people.

Then when they were singing hymns like the ones in the Methodist Church I grew up in, I began having flashbacks. I wondered how my mother would have experienced this. It was a Christian service, but with something "peculiar" going on. I don't think she could have handled it. I was having strong feelings during the service, fighting back tears the whole time. . . .

## FAILED BONDING

I had had bad feelings about our relationship when Chris was growing up. I felt a failure. I couldn't seem to make contact with him. He seemed irritated with me a lot and I'd get irritated with him.

I kept trying to get Chris into playing catch, and he just wasn't interested. So I thought, "Okay, don't lay my trip on him. Let him be where he is."

Later I then tried to get him interested in Boy Scouts. He had no interest in that either. I don't think we went to more than three or four meetings.

The scouts had a father and son overnight that fall. We were in pup tents, and there was an early snow. Chris got sick and had to be taken home during the night. It just seemed like nothing was working. . . .

## BEING HONEST

For a while after finding out, Marilyn and I had a tendency not to talk about it. It was easier to talk about anything else. Finally, we agreed that the subject would be one we would actively bring up. We began to move.

When Chris came home the first time after telling us, he probed about where we were in our understanding. He wanted us to assure him that we totally accepted his homosexuality. We both said we couldn't—that we hadn't made our peace with it yet. We didn't give him anything phony. He had to accept us where we were.

That was one of the first corners we got around. It was a critical step for all of us to stay with reality. Being exactly where we were was the most caring thing we could do. He had been honest with us when he came out and that set the tone for how we had to deal with each other.

At some point I decided that I had to make some kind of adjustment about his gayness. I could not become fixated on my own misery and discomfort. I had to let go of it. I didn't like it, but gradually I decided it was his life.

I've moved to the point where I can deal honestly with Chris. We can be open about one of the heaviest of issues, homosexuality. It's a number one challenge, because I started as far back as anyone.

All the ideas I had of homosexuality were negative. It was something I don't remember ever talking about. My image was that gays were people who picked up sex in the park. It was dirty and was done by people with strange mannerisms. Then I realized that I, myself, was now associated with gayness. My child was into something that repels a lot of people. I'm now part of it.

So, my feelings about homosexuality in general were riding heavily on my shoulders. They were wrapped around me and I had trouble getting them off. . . .

## HANG-UPS AND CHANGES

Perfectionism is a tyranny that I've had trouble shaking. I thought I had to give up all my negative feelings in order to have a good relationship with Chris. But anger and negative feelings are just a part of living. There's always ambivalence. Right now, I say I'll probably always have wishes that he weren't a homosexual. He's without a partner and I often think he will have a lonely kind of battle.

While I still have my hang-ups about homosexuality, I know we also have moved closer to each other. I feel good that Chris and I can hug each other. He now says he wants us to live near him in California. When I think about how much of a failure I felt in relation to Chris when he was growing up, I find these changes remarkable. . . .

[One year later] significant changes have continued to take

place. Until about a year ago I harbored many regrets. I still thought if I had a choice, I would want Chris to be heterosexual. Even after all my involvement in the parents' group, I joined the long line of parents who said, "Of course we wouldn't choose it for our child."

I've gotten away from that, and I'm trying to get in touch with why. I think it has to do with what has happened and with a change of perception about what really has been good for my life and for Chris. But the changes came only after some hard discussions with him.

One summer evening around the fire at our mountain cabin in Colorado, I told Chris of my continuing distaste for the sexual acts between men.

He was hurt that I would come back with statements and feelings out of the old places. It was hard for him to hear me go back to these harsh messages. But he knew they were in me, and he was willing to face the issues once again.

In these tough confrontations with Chris I got into the real nitty-gritty. I can't recount all the details, but as we talked I heard myself realizing truths about sex that I had pushed aside. Chris pointed out that nongays engage in the same sexual behaviors which are condemned for gays, and that therefore the image of "dirty" that I had associated with gay sex was also valid for heterosexual sex.

I became aware that I had resisted acknowledging these facts. I have mixed feelings about the whole sexual revolution. Deeply rooted within me is the traditional western teaching that only heterosexual sex is okay. But I also know that I welcome for myself a wider range of sexual expression, including what I was condemning in gay people. I began to realize how hypocritical I was being. I finally could laugh at myself....

## OPENING MY EYES

I have come to realize that my son's being gay has been a major source of personal liberation for me. I grew up in a conservative, German neighborhood with the message: "Keep in mind what the neighbors will think." I have gradually come to realize how crippling and burdensome that message is. It asked me not to look at the world through my own eyes and not to face the truth about my life as I experienced it. I spent too much of my energy trying to keep up appearances.

If Chris had not been gay, I would have let life cheat me. In a very real sense he rescued me from that. I am freer now to take other risks as I face what I want to do with my life.

It is Chris' nature to be gay. That is the way he came into the world, and the way he is in the world. I would never change him even if I could. He and all the other gay and lesbian children have a right to be here as they are. They can help us expand our lives by widening the range of differences that we can embrace and enjoy.

# A Mother Feels Guilt over Her Daughter's Homosexuality

by Anonymous

> In the 1990s, editor Bryce McDougall compiled an anthology of letters that parents wrote to him describing their reactions to finding out about and coping with the news of their child's homosexuality. The following letter was written by a mother from Adelaide, Australia, who at the time was struggling to come to terms with her daughter's admission that she was a lesbian. In the letter, the mother blames herself for possibly raising her daughter improperly. Now that her daughter has come out, the mother feels only anger that she is the one who is forced to accept her child's "choice," even if it brings so much unhappiness to their relationship. According to McDougall, the mother's bitterness has abated some since the writing of the letter, and she now maintains that her resentment is only a stage that will pass.

My initial feelings of anger and guilt are still with me, despite it being two years since my daughter told me of her homosexuality. I have additional feelings, too, none of which will help any other parent in dealing with this problem, but they just might make them feel that they are not alone in this dreadful mourning.

There's the guilt because my beautiful daughter is flawed. Was it my fault? Did I love her so much that she learned a woman's love is the only worthy thing? Or did I err in teaching her that girls are as good as the boys they're forced to compete with? Should I have let her play the sports she showed talent for, water-polo and cricket? A good mother might have forced her to play with dolls, and sit at home with her knitting and sewing. Blame! It never ends, but love can when reality intrudes.

Anger. Yes, I understand anger, too. Why me? Why can't I hand down to my grandchildren the drawings she did at kindergarten and

---

Bryce McDougall, *My Child Is Gay: How Parents React When They Hear the News*. St. Leonards, Australia: Allen & Unwin, 1998. Copyright © 1998 by Bryce McDougall. All rights reserved. Reproduced by permission.

the sweet little stories she wrote at primary school? She took her sporting trophies with her when she left, and a good thing, too, because if I had a continual reminder of her lifestyle, I'd only have another reason to cry every day.

I can't cope and I doubt that I ever will. Life is meaningless—she taught me that. I wasted my time marrying and producing children. If I hadn't done either, I could have saved myself all this heartbreak. Given my time again, I doubt I'd have children, and I'd do my best never to love anyone more than myself. This, I think, is called bitterness.

Then there's honesty, the hardest of all. I might hate myself for it but I wish she had died instead. What a trivial existence it seems, the life of a gay person. A half-life, with no births or marriages, other than a hypocritical relationship formed in imitation of a procreational couple. Betrayal is all I can see, betrayal of me as a mother. She rejects my beliefs, my principles and my femininity. Why? Was there something so hateful about my love that all she wanted to do was scorn me until the end of my days?

## I DON'T WANT TO LOVE HER

It seems unfair, but I'm not allowed to have any emotion over this. If I do, I'm being manipulative. She won't change her mind, and she made this choice, but guess what? My unhappiness puts pressure on her. So I'm not allowed to be unhappy. A good mother, I'm told, would be thrilled that her daughter has found peace. Perhaps she has, but she's destroyed mine. Since I'm not allowed to feel any emotion, or express my honest thoughts, all I can do is stop loving her. As she has no other choice, neither do I.

Yes, love dies. I tell myself this every day in the hope that it will happen to me. I can't forgive her, I can't respect her and I certainly can't understand her. I don't want to love her any longer.

# A Wife Struggles with the Revelation That Her Husband Is Gay

by Carol Grever

After thirty years of marriage, Carol Grever, a businesswoman and English professor in Boulder, Colorado, found out her husband was gay. Grever had always known that her marital relations were strained, but she had never suspected the reason. Once her husband's secret was revealed, Grever spent five years trying to make the marriage last. In the end, however, she and her husband separated.

In response to the entire ordeal, Grever authored a book on the subject and sought input from other wives who faced the same marital crisis. The following excerpt from that book follows Grever's personal journey from the moment her husband, Jim, confided in her to the point at which she was able to accept the reality of her failed marriage and move on to a sense of independence. Grever relies heavily on journal entries that she wrote as she struggled to cope with her husband's secret life, her resentment that his revelation liberated him but imprisoned her, and her feelings of insecurity about the uncertain future.

When Jim sat on the garden wall with me and told me he had homosexual tendencies, he was in extreme emotional pain. He had been acting on those tendencies for a long time, of course, but had successfully compartmentalized his actions—out of sight, out of mind. He had also successfully deceived me for nearly thirty years. When I asked for a separation that spring, it forced the issue and he began to tell me the truth.

Why didn't I suspect? An entry from my journal shows some of the clues I saw earlier, but didn't comprehend. "All day cleaning winter's debris from the garden, I was thinking about Jim. Here's how it is with Jim and me. After more than thirty years of marriage (maybe twenty-

Carol Grever, *My Husband Is Gay: A Woman's Guide to Surviving the Crisis.* Freedom, CA: The Crossing Press, 2001. Copyright © 2001 by Carol Grever. All rights reserved. Reproduced by permission from The Crossing Press, a division of Ten Speed Press, Berkeley, CA. www.tenspeed.com.

five of which were reasonably happy), I feel really alone. We have less and less in common. Our continuing drive to sell the business is connected to our growing insecurity in our marriage. It would be unthinkable to work so closely together at the office if we ultimately live apart. After our business is gone, what will be left between us? Only history? Convenience? Pride? Is that enough to stay married?

"Jim communicates less and less and seeks companionship away from home. He has his friends; I have mine. His interests are increasingly different from mine and he is obsessed with youth. Flashy clothes and expensive toys excite him. I don't.

"As he pointed out to me during an argument this morning, we never had common interests. He likes movies, I like to read; he likes oldies, I like New Age music; he likes city excitement, I like quiet mountain walks. On and on. No one's to blame—we are who we are. Still, it is depressing for a married couple to work so hard at finding even a few activities we can share and both enjoy.

"As I increasingly look inward, it is less important to keep up the old front, make an impression, or spend time with people I don't care about. My circle of friends narrows but deepens by the year. I'm delegating as much of my responsibility in the business as possible, pulling away from public view, step by step. In contrast, Jim seems compelled to surround himself with crowds of jazzy kids. He dresses like a twenty-year-old, following absurd fads. He dyes his hair and shaves off his graying beard. All of his energy is directed toward the surface. Andy Warhol nailed it: Jim is deeply superficial. I'm sick over our separation of spirit."

If I had even remotely suspected the reason for these changes in my formerly conventional mate, I would not have experienced such utter shock at Jim's disclosure. I was truly unaware. All I knew was that I felt unhappy and somehow abandoned. Fortunately for both of us Jim's genuine anguish touched me so deeply that I responded to his confession with compassion rather than anger. Those first crucial hours allowed us to feel closer again, at least while I adjusted to this new knowledge. We treated each other with concern, able to call on the love that remained. Though I certainly didn't realize it at the time, I was one of the lucky ones. . . .

## TRUSTING THAT THE MARRIAGE WILL WORK

Sharing a secret of this magnitude may create a bond of sympathy and compassion, particularly in the first days after disclosure. This is especially likely where there has been a good measure of mutual love and respect in the marriage....

In my case, there was a dizzying mixture of hope, hurt, and despair, but I desperately wanted our marriage to hold together. My idealism prevailed for a while. In my journal I wrote, "Where from here? My mind reels with the magnitude of this change, but my heart clings to the hope that we can grow beyond our wounds and build a new, truthful relationship. It's clear that we both want to have some kind of life together, but what a bizarre marriage this has become.

"Is a lifetime bond possible, despite our vast differences? The odds are against it, but we have been astonished this weekend at the closeness we suddenly feel. Jim's tears washed away years of secrecy and shame. With his truthfulness this weekend and his solemn promise to continue telling only the truth, Jim has risen, not fallen, in my esteem. This in itself is a miracle.

"For now, then, our plan is to continue counseling jointly and separately to help us adjust to this revelation. Though at this moment I feel no resentment, I fear my anger will build. Will I begin to feel cheated, antagonistic? Will judgment raise its ugly face? Will my present warmth toward Jim turn cold? The path ahead is rocky and shrouded in uncertainty. All I know tonight is that I want to heal my marriage."

My first blush of optimism lasted only several days. Later in the following week, I clung to the hope that truthfulness was a lasting possibility for us. I felt genuine compassion for Jim's life-long necessity to live a lie. "Truth cleanses. After Friday night's catharsis, this weekend took on a closeness Jim and I have not known ever before. His anguished confession did indeed set us free to relax a little and explore meanings. We rested in each other's acceptance.

## HOPE FOR COMPANIONSHIP

"So many questions were answered. Remembered hurts, the enigma of Jim's aloofness, his frequent absences, his flamboyant young friends—it all makes sense now. We talked again and again about his experiences with male sex partners. How sad that all were anonymous except three. Intimacy with a nameless stranger must surely be the abyss of loneliness.

"Perhaps this unaccustomed truthfulness allows us the possibility to build a genuine life together, giving us understanding unknown in our old, separated compartments. I'm overwhelmed with thankfulness for this second chance to have the kind of companionship I've only dreamed about, even if that relationship is asexual. Even if our marriage is different from most, perhaps it can still be solid and loving.

"The other sensation I feel is fatigue. I am very tired physically, as though I'm recovering from a long, debilitating illness. This will pass I'm sure. In the meantime, I intend to take care of myself the best I can—good food, less alcohol, lots of rest, massage. This past year has been the most difficult of my life. May the loneliness and separation begin to heal now."

As much as I tried to sustain it, however, the glow of our newfound intimacy lasted only a short while. . . .

## WANTING TO KNOW EVERYTHING

My curiosity raged, especially at first. Since I knew absolutely nothing about homosexual activities, I pressed for information. Here are some excerpts from my journal during that time. "It has been two days since this turn of fate. For the rest of the Memorial Day weekend, we talked constantly, all day and in the middle of the night. I couldn't get enough information. I asked hundreds of questions. My curiosity about his foreign lifestyle was insatiable. Jim patiently and completely answered every question, though he was sometimes embarrassed.

"How do you find out which places are gay bars?"

"What do you say?"

"How do you know someone else is gay—how can you tell in a crowd?"

"What did you do in those bathhouses?"

"How does it feel when a man touches you?"

Once, when I doubted his claim that he could locate the gay community in any city, he responded by looking up the Gay and Lesbian Community Center in the Denver white pages. He told me that most major cities have such listings. He dialed the help line and I listened in fascination as he said that he was in Denver on a business trip and was staying at the downtown Marriott. He inquired about friendly places near the hotel, writing down addresses of two bars and a bathhouse. His voice was different on the phone—a chatty, soft, intimate purr. I had never heard him speak that way. As he hung up, he handed me his notes and simply smiled. . . .

For months after Jim came out to me, we thought we could rebuild our former marital relationship. This struggle created a dilemma for us both. We were increasingly certain that he would not be able to resist other men. It was summertime, and Jim spent more and more time with his male friends. He took more trips out of town and I spent more time alone. I had a deep sense of dislocation and isolation. I was scared for us both. After painful consideration, I took a leap and offered him the gift of my consent. I wrote in my journal, "Since we are both certain that Jim will again act on his homosexual urges, I gave him my blessing to satisfy those needs outside our marriage, with only two conditions: Practice only safe sex and tell me no lies. We'll have no games, no recrimination—just honesty. He agreed to stop cruising gay bars and to swear off momentary encounters in toilets with strangers. Those practices are just too dangerous—for both of us. Jim showed increasing relief as we talked. He can have it all now, protected socially by the cover of a traditional-looking marriage.". . .

## FUTURE UNCERTAINTY

My own central emotion, after the stark reality of my situation became clear, was deep sadness. It came in great waves, ebbing and flowing like the tide. Everything Jim and I had accomplished together no longer counted; our bright future plans were never to be realized. We would not enjoy a peaceful retirement together. We would not travel the world together. We would not know the security of mutual, loving support. We would not grow old together in our cozy home. When this became depressingly clear, I experienced huge mood swings. I would cope pretty well for days at a time, then hit what I came to call a black hole. Each time another crisis struck, I experienced terrible despair, like a freefall into an abyss of terrifying darkness.

As an example, for weeks Jim and I had planned to go to the local dinner theater. Nervous to be going out with my own husband (now that I knew more about him), I wore my prettiest dressy outfit, a simple black dress with a gold paisley jacket. I spent extra time fussing with my hair and makeup. I wanted everything to be perfect that evening. (I suppose that I was still trying to impress or seduce him.) Everything seemed fine as we enjoyed dinner and a good performance of *Cabaret*.

But afterward, it wasn't so pleasant. I described the ordeal in my journal. "When we returned home, I was again abruptly overwhelmed by the sadness of our probable separation. I dropped into a black cave of desperate despair. I love Jim. I really don't want to lose him. But now it seems inevitable. Since this whole drama began, I have been afraid that if I ever let go of my tight hold on my emotions, if I ever start to weep, I might never stop crying. I've dammed up floods of tears.

"But I did let go last night. I cried bitterly all night. Everything I ever wanted is out of my grasp. Why? Why! My ribs ache today from those terrible, tearing sobs. My whole face feels raw. I hate this fearful uncertainty and pray that my radical moods will somehow level. I can't stand this ambivalence!"

## FROM ANGER TO A BETTER FUTURE

Right after that particular emotional crash, Jim left with four men for yet another boating vacation at Lake Powell. On Monday, I was bombarded at work with decisions and responsibility I was supposed to share with him. I resented the fact that he was working only about half time and spending so many days playing at the lake. Why should I have to pick up the slack?

Midmorning, I attended graveside services for a friend's father, who had been an avid fisherman and outdoorsman. I was touched by sweet, homely eulogies by his old buddies, praising a man who was plain-spoken and simple like my own dad. I grieved for my friend and her father and for my father—and for myself.

Teary-eyed, I returned to the office where I immediately received a long-distance call from Jim. He phoned from Bullfrog Marina to say that he was having such a great time at the lake, he and the guys had decided to stay over another few days. I calmly hung up the phone, then exploded inside. Jim had it all and I did not! I was flooded with rage, thinking all Jim thought about was entertaining himself. Having fun, especially with 'the boys,' seemed like it was his top priority. It made me furious! That night, still in a rage, I wrote: "What is he bringing to the table in our attempt to heal? He confessed that he's gay. Is that his only responsibility? Is that enough? Now he's free to go about his unspeakable business without censure. Can he now run around with his queer buddies, blaming infidelity on his nature and feeling guiltless because I know? How much do I not know? He lied to me for thirty years. I had no clue that he was doing so. How can I trust him now?

"What do I have? I get the leftovers of his energy—at work, at home, in bed, on social occasions. I'm always second in line. Where does he get off thinking that because he told me the truth about being gay, he's suddenly exonerated, free to keep on with his swinging life, while his little bird at home waits under his table to peck up the crumbs? I'm hurt. I'm sad. I'm furious tonight."

Notice that sadness led to this particular bout of anger. Like kites, driven up and down by capricious gusts, Jim and I skittered through many months like this with alternate times of hope and despair, optimism and frigid fear—and inevitable anger. For us both, the closet was a lonely, discouraging trap. And my recurring black hole threatened my mental and physical health for years afterward. . . .

Is there any hope? Will this horrible ordeal ever end? For most women who have walked this path, the answer is yes. Their predictable, necessary period of anger is the darkest night before the dawning light of recovery. The worst is past because the woman's very anger is a signal that she has turned the corner and has begun to think of her own needs. She can then open to new possibilities and take responsibility for her own well-being. So the arduous process of digging out of the black hole of anger and despair often brings clearer vision to see a better future.

# CHAPTER 3

## Self-Acceptance and Identity

SOCIAL ISSUES FIRSTHAND

# Accepting My Body and Myself

by Anna Mills

> In high school and college, Anna Mills suffered from an eating disorder that made her extremely conscious of her body image. She believed that controlling her weight would ensure that her boyfriends would remain loyal and attracted to her. In her early twenties, though, she discovered that her self-abuse was just an outward expression of an internal struggle over her own identity. For years Mills had adhered to the dictates of a straight society while secretly suppressing her attraction toward women. Only after reading some feminist writers who opened her eyes to the liberation of feminine identity did Mills accept her homosexuality. In the following narrative, Mills explains how her newfound freedom gave her the perspective to banish her eating disorder and finally feel comfortable with her own body.
>
> Anna Mills was twenty-three years old when she wrote this story of coming to terms with her own identity. At that time she was working for Americorps in an inner-city school near Palo Alto, California.

I had an eating disorder in high school. Like millions of American girls, I hated my body. I ate compulsively, and believed I could never be normal. I was achingly envious of thin, attractive women.

I sat hunched over my books, eating piece after piece of buttered toast, unable to taste the bread. I lay down with an aching stomach, feeling the extra folds of skin, the soft flesh. I got up to run for miles, my legs pounding, determined to be clean. At school I watched a fellow actress in the dressing room as she posed in her black lingerie costume. Her slim curves, her long blond hair, the silk straps over her tan skin. Unreachable beauty.

I was fascinated when men liked me. I believed that by controlling my weight, I could ensure a boyfriend's loyalty. If he drifted away, I knew he had finally noticed my body was too big. If he stayed, I was

Anna Mills, "Secret Hungers," *Revolutionary Voices*, edited by Amy Sonnie. Los Angeles: Alyson Publications, 2000. Copyright © 2000 by Anna Mills. Reproduced by permission.

hungry for sex. His desire made me feel alive. I couldn't name my own needs or desires, much less assert them. I could not touch him unless he touched me. Part of me stayed numb while we kissed for hours. Sometimes I felt waves of sickness. Sometimes I was drawn into passion like a whirlpool in darkness. Through all this, I was positive of one thing: One day I would lose the weight and begin to glow.

## SOMETHING WAS WRONG

As my eating obsession raged on in college, feminist accounts of eating disorders reassured me. I was suffering from issues of body image and sense of self that affect all women in our society. Because women are treated as sex objects, I learned, we are often alienated from our sexuality and from our desires. That made sense to me. I knew there was something wrong with the way I kept sneaking and stealing food, eating boxes of cookies at a time and hating myself. But I also knew there was something deeply wrong with my passive, fearful sexuality. I latched onto feminist writers as my liberation.

I used all the tools I could find to develop my sense of self and my ability to communicate. I learned to speak, through therapy, support groups, writing stories, in journals, arguing in classes, talking for hours on the phone—desperately trying to connect to others, to understand my feelings and needs and make myself heard. I learned that I wanted to be big, to take up space, to rage. I slowly began to transform my hunger into language.

## HAPPINESS WAS NOW POSSIBLE

Throughout the process of recovery, I never questioned my sexuality. Lesbians were the "Other," and the idea of wanting a woman was an empty space. It amazes me that my imagination was so controlled by my culture that I could not recognize something so central to my being. But the long process of learning to speak and learning to take up space had prepared me.

Something shifted inside me. Something light, crazy, and joyous took hold of me. I felt like I was dancing through my life. I came out, and it was as if a heavy, dark cloud had been lifted from me. A happiness I had only glimpsed before was now possible. I stared at women on the street, in my classes, in movies.

And I noticed a strange correlation. I still felt an electric response to women's bodies. Now, however, I named it differently. Instead of envy and despair, it was a flash of heat and recognition. "She's so sexy," I would whisper, then hug myself and smile.

The change was dizzying. I came out to friends, family, and to my whole campus in the span of two weeks. The threat of my eating obsession disappeared. It would never return.

## LINKED ANXIETIES

I had prayed for years for someone to tell me, plainly and simply, what my eating disorder was about. No theory suggested that shame about my body, my needs, and desires might be shame about my queer sexuality. None suggested that envy of women might be a cover for desire. Those suggestions may be too threatening to straight feminists. Most women suffer from similar anxiety, guilt, and food obsession, and all women are constrained by compulsory heterosexuality. Perhaps food and body-image obsession are a secret language for all women. They speak a rebellion, a refusal to fit mind and soul into the role of the perfect straight girl. They speak women's hunger for more intimate, physical, primary relationships to other women. Their rebellion is silent—it draws attention to the symptom and not the cause.

As I came out, I began to feel that my body belonged to me. I stopped scrutinizing it for ugliness or sexiness. I stopped feeling like an object, and more like a body in relation to other women's bodies. When I talked with a woman I was attracted to, I could feel the energy in me and between us, in our words, our postures, our smiles—a link across empty space. I developed innumerable tiny crushes. I'd had crushes when I was straight, but they made me feel inadequate and wistful. With my new crushes, I didn't stop to worry about measuring up. I prized my feelings and talked about the crush as if it were an accomplishment.

My residual feelings of guilt about eating evaporated. I would still sit down and eat a box of cookies at a stretch fairly frequently. But I usually let myself shrug off the complex, painful emotions that go with a binge. They seemed like a waste of energy. The guilt and secrecy were unnecessary.

## SUBLIME IMPERFECTION

I began to take pride in the fact that I would never be the perfect, pretty, docile straight girl—treasured by my family and by men, celebrated by society. As a young white woman in a racist society, I grew up with this fantasy of white womanhood—that I was to be cherished, protected and admired. I lived in a rich, white suburb where I was cushioned by privilege. We never talked about the neighboring town of people of color; we knew very few people who lived there. Yet we believed we were progressive and pro civil rights. I was blind to the racism around me and inside me, just as I was to the homophobia and sexism.

I am just beginning to understand how my whiteness affected my eating disorder and my gender role. I am just beginning to see how I can fight not just my own oppression, but also other kinds of blindness and hate.

I may never be that "perfect" girl, but I know I am someone much stronger and happier—a woman-loving baby dyke. Not diseased by homophobia, but coming into my own, coming out of my nightmare cocoon.

# The Choice of a Gay Identity

by Jordan Roth

> In the following article, writer and theatrical producer Jordan Roth discusses the concept of choice in the formation of gay identity. In Roth's view, one must first differentiate between homosexuality (the physical attraction to members of the same sex) and being gay (the acknowledgment of a specific lifestyle) in order to understand the role of choice in the matter. He argues that homosexuality is no more a matter of choice than height or hair color. A homosexual cannot choose to deny the physical impulse to be attracted to members of the same sex. However, he insists, the way a homosexual lives his or her life is indeed a choice. Choosing to be gay means deciding to reject society's misguided attempts to judge and change homosexuals. It means choosing to create a community that lives with pride, dignity, kinship, and love.

If you could choose to not be gay, would you?

Wait. Think about it for a second. The knee-jerk response is to assume battle positions and scream, "*It's not a choice!*" But that's not the question—though it may well reveal the answer. Maybe our rush to defensiveness exposes the implied conclusion: "Because if it were, I wouldn't choose it."

Scientists have been working overtime lately to prove what our bodies tell us every day: Sexual preference is a biological fact. The research shows that an identical twin of a gay person is twice as likely to be gay as a fraternal twin, that the brain anatomy of a gay man is measurably different from that of a straight man, that lesbians have finger lengths and blink reflexes that are more similar to those of men than of women, and that a man is more likely to be gay the more older brothers he has because of readjusted hormonal balances in his mother's womb. These studies all point to the conclu-

Jordan Roth, "Do We Choose to Be Gay?" www.Advocate.com, February 12, 2004. Copyright © 2004 by Jordan Roth. Reproduced by permission.

sion that homosexuality is either completely, or at least in some significant part, biologically determined.

It's all good news. It's all what we feel is true. It's all what we want to hear: Being gay is not a choice, so you can't try to change me and you can't discriminate against me.

But what do we lose by insisting that being gay is not a choice? What do we lose by placing our identities out of our own control? What does it do to us to remove ourselves from our identity, to render ourselves powerless in our own selves?

## DIFFERENTIATING HOMOSEXUALITY FROM GAY IDENTITY

To say that we have no choice in being gay is to say that being gay is only the desire to love another man or another woman, that it is only about sex. But being gay is not simply a desire for sex with the same sex. That's *homosexual*. *Gay* is an identity, a culture, a community, a place. And while we are born homosexual, we choose to be gay. We must build the strength and develop the courage to forge our lives as gay people, to create a space in which we can define our lives as fundamentally and necessarily gay. And that is something we choose to do every day. It is a choice we may struggle with, a choice we make sacrifices for, and a choice we fight for. To deny our active involvement in that choice is to deny our active involvement in that struggle, in those sacrifices, in that fight. And to deny our active involvement is to deny our right to be proud.

Gay pride has always confused me a little, even from atop a float dancing down Fifth Avenue. Proud of what? What did I do to be proud of? If being gay is just a biological fact about me, no different from my height or natural hair color, why does being gay warrant a parade?

Granted, if the whole world had been screaming for hundreds of years that my height was sick and wrong and immoral, and the whole world was constantly threatening to strap me to a medieval stretching machine to crank me to my rightful height, a counteractive Height Parade to scream back at them would be a relief. There are certainly a frightening number of people out there wielding medieval straightening machines just salivating over the chance to undo whatever trauma or confusion they believe to be the root of our gayness.

But that can't be the whole point of our pride. We can't live our entire lives defensively. We can't forever think of ourselves in reaction to or opposed to what others think of us. At some point we need to realize that we are proud—truly proud—not just because someone else thinks we shouldn't be, but because we are.

Why? Because we had a choice. We could have chosen to live in the shadows. We could have chosen a life of denial and deception. We could have hollowed out our insides and vigilantly stood guard against our natural desires every time they poked up from beneath the surface. That too is a choice. Not a comfortable choice, not a painless choice, but a choice nonetheless—a choice that many have made—a choice we could have made, but we did not.

## GAY IDENTITY IS A CHOICE

The desire to love another man, to love another woman, we do not choose. It may not even be completely our choice when we act on these desires. But living our lives and creating our identities based on these desires, based on the nurturing and celebration of these desires, is our choice. And it is a difficult choice to make. We could have accepted what we were told about ourselves, about who we should be and what we should not do or feel. Going in search of another answer is grueling and treacherous. To bushwhack through the dogma and the tauntings and the lessons carved into our bodies by hundreds of years of tradition and emerge at a clearing of calm and beauty takes sweat and muscle and resilience. To make that effort is a hard choice, the choice less traveled. And the fact that we make that choice is something of which we can be truly proud.

Proud that we are creating a community of choice. Proud that we are where we are and that we're going where we're going. Proud that we are each continuing the daily battle against self-doubt and self-destruction as best we can. Proud of that 19-year-old boy who must have trudged through land mines and mud slides and bloody battlefields to get from Wherever, USA, to 22nd Street, but he's here now, and he just looked up at the sky and smiled. Proud that we are part of a culture, a legacy, that includes the words of Tony Kushner, the fire of Larry Kramer, and the voice of Harvey Fierstein. Proud that we are standing on the shoulders of those who loved before us. And proud of them and the choices they made.

To be clear, this is not to say that there is only one way to live a gay life. The group of tanned, tank top–clad guys brunching on Eighth Avenue are not more gay than the man who lives simply in the mountains of Colorado. Nor is it to suggest that living a gay life means living a life consumed by pursuing and having sex. A gay person who has sex very infrequently if at all is still gay and living a gay life. Rather, this is about a gay identity, which is fundamentally based on finding comfort, love, kinship, beauty, and yes, sex, in people of the same sex. This is about the choices we make and the way we choose to build our lives based on that comfort, love, kinship, beauty, and sex; that we choose to make those things intrinsic and essential to who we are and how we live, not simply incidental. This is about the way we choose to live our lives: as gay people.

## IS DISCRIMINATION JUSTIFIABLE?

But if being gay—or rather if *living* gay—is a choice, doesn't that mean that the Right is right, that we can unchoose, unlearn, be ungayed? No. There are two answers to those who would change us and come at us wielding their straightening machines: We cannot be changed because we had no choice, and we cannot be changed because we have chosen. It's not that we can't; it's that we won't. We won't go back into hiding. We won't accept your idea that we are sick. We won't turn our backs on each other and the lives we are creating together. We won't deny ourselves our identity. Because we don't want to, and we're that strong.

And no, the fact that we can but won't is not justification for our legalized discrimination. Our sexual desires are a biological reality just like our sex and our race. The fact that we can choose to hide or deny those desires—unlike sex or race—but that we refuse to do so provides no grounds for discriminating against us. Our religion, for instance, is not beyond our control, not an innate fact about ourselves; we can choose to change religions or abandon religion altogether. Nonetheless, freedom of religion and freedom from discrimination based on religion is an essential tenant of our nation's foundation. The fact that we can choose what religious doctrine to place our faith in does not mean we can be discriminated against on the basis of that choice. Similarly, the fact that we can choose to live a life celebrating our true emotional and sexual desires does not mean that we can be discriminated against on the basis of that choice.

We have a choice. We have chosen: life, this life, more life. And we will defend that choice and our right to make it with all that is strong and true and brave within us. We are warriors of spirit. We will smash the straightening machines simply by living, by choosing our lives. By reaching out for our lover's hand as we cross the street, by finding comfort, love, kinship, beauty, and sex with one another, and yes, by marching the parade route of pride every year—not as acts of necessity or defiance but as acts of choice. And we will not rob ourselves of the pride we feel—the pride we have earned—at having made this choice by claiming it was never our choice to begin with.

# Diary of a Gay Priest

by Bruce J. Simpson

> Bruce J. Simpson is an archbishop of the Benedictine Order of St. John the Beloved. He lives and works in Pennsylvania, ministering especially to gays who have otherwise felt unwelcomed by the restrictive views of the Catholic Church. Simpson is a homosexual and has written about some of his trials and joys as a priest in his autobiography, *The Gay Face of God*. Some of that story was also published in a 1999 column in *Genre* magazine, from which the following selection was taken.
>
> In his account, Simpson describes how he worked as a police officer before answering the call to enter the priesthood. Once inside the Catholic seminary, Simpson learned that homosexuality pervades the order, but the majority of gay priests remain closeted for fear of being expelled. Simpson kept his own secret for some time, but he eventually confessed it to an archbishop who was not sympathetic. Unwilling to bend to the rigid rules or remain under scrutiny, Simpson left the seminary and returned to secular life. The calling, however, was still strong, and he eventually joined an Old Catholic order. Old Catholicism is a sect of the Catholic Church that has more lenient views on contraception, does not believe in papal infallibility, and does not require its priests to be celibate, among other distinctions. In his new church, Simpson rose rapidly through the ranks. As an archbishop, Simpson now carries on a crusade against religious intolerance—especially as directed toward the gay community.

I was baptized a Roman Catholic at 21 and believed it to be the religion that answered my spiritual needs, but little did I know what was in store. My vocation has always been with me, though understanding its meaning took years to discover. It is hard to describe what a "vocation," or "calling" is to someone who has never experienced it. It is much like a gentle tug at one's soul. I never encountered burning bushes or voices from heaven or e-mail with a divine return address. God is spirit and talks to our souls, which are the

---

Bruce J. Simpson, "My Heart Speaks: Diary of a Gay Priest," *Genre*, July 1999. Copyright © 1999 by Genre Publishing, Inc. Reproduced by permission.

spirits within each of us. I found that the more I ignored this gentle tugging, the more persistent the calling became. All of my previous experience had been as a member of a U.S. Air Force helicopter nuclear-response team and as a security specialist. So to consider even starting down the road to priesthood was an alien concept, for my dream had been to be a police officer.

## SECULAR PURSUITS

In fact, I continued to ignore the calling and became a policeman in Reading, Pennsylvania, and started college majoring in liberal arts. It was during this time that I met my life partner Jack. He lived next to me in Reading, and on the way to work one day, I spotted him and said to myself, "That one's for me." A couple months later, we were lovers. We moved to New Hampshire, where I continued college and joined the local police department. It was there that I was baptized and became friends with several priests, all of who were gay. I moved to Florida after a year, entered the University of Central Florida and finished my degree, obtaining a B.A. in law.

After graduation, Jack and I moved to Maryland just outside of Washington, D.C. My feelings about my vocation never dimmed and in fact became stronger. Still, I resisted. I was appointed to the District Court of Maryland as a commissioner, which in other jurisdictions is called a magistrate. After a while, I left that job and reentered the police force, where the urge to join the priesthood became more than I could resist.

## ENTERING THE SEMINARY

I had just been named Police Officer of the Year when I decided to enter the seminary to commence studies for the priesthood. The most difficult thing about this process was leaving Jack in order to move to the seminary. I had been accepted at Mt. St. Mary's Seminary in Emmittsburg, Maryland. We sold our house and paid all our bills, and I released Jack from any commitment to me. I gave him his freedom to pursue another man or to move away if he desired. And so the journey began.

I still remember my first week in the seminary. I felt lonely and missed Jack terribly. On top of this, I was assigned a roommate whom I didn't particularly care for. Then the academics started. As I sat on the front porch trying to read *Summa Theologica* by St.

Thomas Aquinas, reading the same page over and over, not understanding any of what I was reading, I began to wonder what I had done to myself, my life and my partner.

Prayer life at the "Mount," as it was called, was very important and became a source of solace and comfort. We were strongly encouraged to be present for morning prayer, which began at 7 A.M., followed by breakfast and then classes. My saving grace in these early days was a priest named Anthony Manochio, the "House" spiritual director, who also became my personal spiritual director. He was one of the most pious, prayerful, understanding men of God I have ever known. He is now deceased, and the world and the Mount are a sadder place for his absence. I confided from the very beginning in Fr. Manochio. I told him I was gay and that I had left a partner behind to enter the Mount. What impressed me the most was that he was genuinely concerned about Jack as well as me. Later on, when Jack would visit me at the Mount, he came to know Fr. Manochio.

## LIFE AT THE MOUNT

I drew strength from the daily prayer life, which included morning prayer, mass, evening prayer and, on Sundays, night prayer, which was my favorite with the exception of mass. On Sunday nights, we chanted the "Divine Office" back and forth in the chapel, alternating between the left and right pews. The exposition of the "Blessed Sacrament" took place, and one seminarian was chosen to assist the rector of the seminary in the ceremony. I had the honor a couple of times and was deeply moved to the very core of my being. I, and many others, would sometimes leave on a natural high, fully in touch with the spiritual part of my existence. The rector, Msgr. McGiness, now also deceased, became a good friend that year. We would play handball together with Fr. Manochio and another seminarian. During one of my brief bouts of "Have I done the right thing?" Msgr. McGiness said to me, "Bruce, I would be very comfortable with you at my side praying me into heaven as I died." I will never forget that conversation.

As for gay men, the seminary was full of us. But at the Mount, celibacy was practiced by a majority, including me. That was also difficult to get used to. I was surrounded by gorgeous guys, many of whom were gay, and could not make sexual contact or conversation with any of them. I got to the point where I could have eaten the paint off the walls. I went from having regular sex with my partner of 10 years to nothing. Shower time, and "custody of the eyes," was most difficult.

During the first year, we were required to go on a retreat in northern New Jersey. We each had a one-man cabin, and we could not talk to one another. One day, all we ate was bread and water. There was all-night exposition, with a rotation of one man per hour staying awake with the Blessed Sacrament. It was January, it had snowed, and it was cold. This was one of the more challenging retreats I had ever been on. What made it strange was that, every night at dinner, all of us would start laughing. Someone would begin, and then the rest of us would join in, all laughing at nothing. We were told that this usually happened.

We had nothing to do but pray, read the Divine Office and think. One of the men I was most attracted to, a short blond guy, was also on the retreat. My thoughts drifted to him from time to time as we took walks together without talking. I think he knew but did not care that I was gay. For all I knew, he could have been gay as well.

## MYSTICAL EXPERIENCE

At the end of the spring semester, I was assigned to St. Matthew's Cathedral in Washington, D.C., where I lived and worked for the summer. I assisted the Archbishop of Washington at all major masses and was in charge of the sacristy. It was during morning prayer, which I performed by myself in the cathedral, that I had what I can only describe as a mystical experience. For what seemed like an hour but was in reality only a few seconds, I felt I had been transported back in time to an ancient Jewish temple. As I looked up toward the ceiling, I saw what appeared to be smoke and sensed a feeling of antiquity. I very much felt as if I were in an ancient Jewish temple. The experience left me with goose bumps and an extreme peacefulness unlike any I had felt before. This was the highlight of my stay at the cathedral—where many other things were less than desirable.

The rector of the cathedral locked all the food supplies each night, so if a priest were hungry, he could not get anything to eat in his own house. It was positively medieval. It was also during this time that I came to know the high and powerful of the Roman Catholic Church, and I became less and less impressed with the men who held these offices. The Vatican secretary of state was the main celebrant at mass one day. During the traditional handshake of

## SELF-ACCEPTANCE AND IDENTITY

peace, he refused to give the shake to anyone below the rank of cardinal. The lowly seminarians who stood right behind him were ignored completely.

Another event stands out in my memory from my time at the cathedral. One day, a woman came in and said, "Father, I need to speak with you," to which I replied that I was only a seminarian and not yet ordained. She said it did not matter. She looked haggard and as if she were yearning for something. So we sat down in the cathedral, and she proceeded to tell me that she was a lesbian, that her lover had just left her and that she felt God was punishing her for being gay. She had stopped eating and drinking. I told her what was in my heart and mind about being a lesbian or a gay man. I told her God did not care; He treated people that way. I told her it was silly to blame God for her breakup, just as it would be silly to blame God for all the divorces in the straight world. I told her that she was a good person and that she needed to get something to eat and drink at once, then come back to the cathedral and say a prayer of thanksgiving to God for making her who she was. Her face lit up, and a kind of peace descended upon her. She thanked me, hugged me and left. I noticed about an hour later that she had come back and was in prayer at the altar. It was not church policy what I told her, for what I offered her would not have been said to her by a priest reciting the party line. I spoke what was in my soul and what I believe God wanted me to say to her. This was the moment of my realization that the church had to change its thoughts on gays and lesbians. I was determined to make a difference, but little did I know what was coming.

## THE CONSERVATIVE ARCHBISHOP

After my stay at the cathedral, I was transferred from the Mount to Theological College at Catholic University of America for the next year of study. This was like going from a monastery to a real undergraduate college, where sex was more prevalent. Prayer life was almost nonexistent on a formal basis, and it was up to us to maintain it. During this time, I continued to assist the Archbishop at major liturgical events and was invited to dinner in his private residence by members of his immediate staff, with whom I had become close friends. This closeness made a subsequent event all the more painful.

During my yearly formal review and meeting with the Archbishop he asked why I had not married the girl that the press talked about my leaving when I entered the seminary. The Archbishop had seen a couple of newspaper stories about "Cop of the Year Enters Seminary" that had been published after I left for the Mount. Being naive and believing one should not lie to one's superiors, I told the Archbishop that my love was for a man, not a woman. While capping his pen, he said, "Well, Bruce, I don't know if I can ordain you now." He then went on to tell me that he did not believe the concept of celibacy applied to gay men because it denoted a lack of marital and sexual union between a man and a woman, not two men. He was also concerned that I would be in his rectories with his pastors. I felt like responding, "Have you seen your pastors lately?" But then he asked something that I feel was reprehensible. He requested that I allow my spiritual director at the Mount, and the priest psychiatrist, who had cleared me for the seminary, to drop their confidentiality vows so that he could question them. Needless to say, I was stunned. I was supposed to go to dinner with him and the other seminarians from Washington that night but refused. The Archbishop sent someone to check on me to see if I were all right, and later on, I found out that a seminarian had jumped from the roof of the seminary in Rome when the Archbishop was rector there over this same type of incident. (I guess he didn't want me to do a half gainer from the roof of Theological College.) I felt that the Archbishop had not the faintest idea of what sexuality and human love were all about. This man, having been rewarded by Rome for his loyalty and ultraconservatism, is now Cardinal James Hickey.

## LEAVING THE SEMINARY

Even though the Archbishop said he would put off a decision on ordaining me until the end of the following semester, I decided there was only one decision I could make. I resigned at the end of that semester. In my letter of resignation, I told the Archbishop that I had given up everything but my dignity to enter the seminary. I went on to say that I would not give that up now. I was brokenhearted, devastated and deeply depressed at having to leave the seminary. The Catholic Church provides no transition assistance for those who leave, so, I was unemployed in my early thirties.

The best thing to happen, however, was that my partner Jack had waited for me. He had not found another man, and in fact he had not even dated. Jack told me, "I knew you would be back one day as my lover again." How right he was.

For the next few years, I maintained a reduced prayer life, remained mildly depressed and held such jobs as chief of security for all high-rise office buildings in downtown Houston, hotel security chief, bodyguard to the royal family of Saudi Arabia and District Court commissioner. Finally, in 1988, I began working for the federal government. I ended up in collections for the Department of Labor and rose to become chief of special collections. In 1996, I transferred to the Department of the Treasury, where I became chief of the debt-collection section for nontax debt. I retired on disability last year because of back and knee problems.

## ORDAINED

But I soon discovered that the vocation was still with me—and strong once again. God was not yet finished with me, nor had He given up. I became more depressed at the calling's insistence and the seeming lack of opportunity to fulfill it. Then I discovered "Old Catholicism" which was Catholic in theology but which had broken from Rome in 1889. I checked into it and found it to be a very legitimate form of Catholicism, one that did not have the hangups of Rome and the requirement of celibacy. I applied to one of the branches of Old Catholicism in New Hampshire and, after completing a course of study, was ordained as a deacon in December 1996. I became a priest in July 1997. It took 10 years from the time I left the seminary to be ordained a deacon. My joy was almost overwhelming, but nothing compared to celebrating mass for the first time as a priest. To hold the host in my hands and repeat the words "Take this all of you and eat it, this is my body which will be given up for you" was, and still is, indescribable. The first time I heard someone's confession, granted absolution for very grievous sins and saw relief and thankfulness on the person's face, I knew that being a conduit for God was meant for me. The Lord has given me certain gifts, which I try to use as best I can. One gift, however, that He chose not to give me is the gift of a singing voice. I sing very little, much to the relief of my congregation.

In December 1998, I was called to the episcopacy and was consecrated a bishop the following month. At my consecration, I announced that I was dedicating my episcopacy to those who have been hurt by religion and to the lesbian and gay community. I believe that God has set me on the path to minister to those who are outcasts, just as Jesus ministered to those who were the outcasts of His day. If I had become a Roman Catholic priest, I would have come into direct conflict with the leaders of the church and probably resigned rather than perpetuate the oppression of gays and lesbians.

## REACHING THE GOSPEL

Let it never be said that this bishop, or the Western Orthodox Catholic Church, ever turned his back on a person for being unworthy of receiving the gifts of the sacraments of the church. I am a servant of God's people, just as all other bishops, priests and deacons. Since becoming bishop, I have testified before the Maryland House Judiciary Committee in support of hate-crimes legislation and equal protection laws for gays and lesbians. I encountered open hostility from one legislator who was also a Baptist pastor. God must have been with me that day, as people later told me that they had never seen anyone able to shut him up. I now keep an eye open for social injustice toward gay people everywhere in the United States. As a successor to the apostles, it is my duty to intervene and to teach the truth of the Gospel—not the mistranslations that are used to keep the gay community suffering. My faith tells me that one day, all in the gay community will find a true place among the churches of the land. This will be the start of acceptance from the larger public, since many use religion as a reason to hate us.

# A Transsexual Struggles for a True Identity

by Alison Lade

The following story was posted to the Web site ComingOutStories.com. In it, Alison, a preoperation transsexual—that is, a man who has yet to have a sex-change operation—begins by giving a brief account of his childhood yearnings to be a girl and his subsequent crossdressing experiences as a preadolescent and teenager. Alison confides that his mother had caught him dressing up in her clothes and branded him a pervert. From that moment on, Alison struggled with his desires to be a girl and his need to please and fit in with those around him.

As Alison matured into his college years, he found more freedom to dress as a woman, but he still suffered guilt and even faced rejection from some of those closest to him. Trying to find his identity, he experimented sexually with both men and women, and he sought acceptance in the gay community. None of these efforts provided the solace he was looking for, and he is still working through his identity issues. But as Alison concludes, accepting himself and coming out to more and more friends has proved overall to be a positive and healthy experience.

I guess the best place to start would be my earliest memories and then work my way forward, eh? Oh yeah, hi. I'm Alison. Born in '75. At this writing I am pre-op M2F TS [male-to-female transsexual who has yet to have surgery to change his gender]. Also at this writing I am out to just about everyone. But it hasn't always been this way.

Let's take a trip back in time. . . .

Two Rivers, Wisconsin, 1975. I was born. My mother had hoped that I would be a girl. After being born, the family moved down the road to Manitowoc. Fortunately they did not forget to pack me.

Some time before I [can remember], my mother and sister, after secretly wishing for another girl in the family, dress me in baby girl clothes and take a picture. My mother will show me this picture

Alison Lade, "Alison's Story," www.comingoutstories.com, 2003. Copyright © 2003 by Alison Lade. Reproduced by permission of the publisher and author.

many years later. It's funny how you should be careful of what you wish for. . . .

Somewhere around age 7, I always knew I was different. I never did relate to the boys much, and I always did yearn to be playing with the girls at recess. But no, I had to play games of athletic skill with the guys. Surprisingly enough, I was good at it. I guess if you can't beat 'em, join 'em. But I always did look over at the monkey bars longingly and wish. Eventually my wishes did come true and I would spend less time with the guys and more time with the girls. Sheer bliss! I had more fun, and my clothes wouldn't get dirty or ripped. So really, I don't know why my mom would object.

## FIRST INKLINGS

Summer time, one year (I assume age 7), I was at home, alone, watching TV. I was glued to it. I loved game shows, and I loved talk shows. Geraldo Rivera was the man! . . . One day [his] show was titled "Crossdressers and the women who love them." "What's a crossdresser?" I asked myself. So yearning for knowledge, I stayed and watched. Intently. Oddly enough, after that show I ran up to my parents' bedroom and went searching. Jackpot! Feminine galore. Anything and everything one could possibly need. And it's all at my disposal. Being one who wanted to find out what it was really like, I grabbed some things from her dresser and put them on.

Woah. Did you ever do something in your life and you felt a "click" inside your head? Like something you could never figure out just instantly became clear? That was my "click." I already knew what to do to make myself a girl. Wear these clothes, find some way to make the figure look right, and there you go. At the time, all I had were socks, so those would have to do. This was also before I figured out what to do with "it." You all know what "it" is, and "it" decided it wanted to annoy me. So I did what any transgender M2F would do, I shoved "it" back to where it came from . . . so to speak. I would eventually find out this was called "tucking." "It" will become a major annoyance in my life because it would try to ruin the smooth female form I was trying to achieve. I didn't like "it," and I put myself through much pain to get "it" to not interfere, including some clever gadgetry, but I'll get to that later.

This day I also learned how important it was to cover my tracks. One item out of place could spell disaster. See, I already knew there was something different about me, and I knew the general public

## SELF-ACCEPTANCE AND IDENTITY

(especially my family) did not approve of this. So being covert became a skill and an art.

Throughout the summer I would continue dressing whenever my family was not at home. Each day I would try something new. A different outfit. Jewelry. Hair things. Pantyhose. Shoes. You get the idea. Each day I tried to become more and more feminine. And each day I was happy with that day's progress and wondered about what else I could do. Until . . .

One evening I was using the bathroom downstairs. This is where my mom kept her makeup. So I started to look through it. Looking at the powder and foundation and lipstick. Tons of lipstick. I always wondered what it was like to wear lipstick, so I tried some on. Why my mother had blue lipstick, I had no idea. Why I chose blue lipstick, I have no earthly clue. Maybe I was curious as to how blue lipstick looked on someone. Maybe it was my inner drag queen talking? Who knows. Staring at myself with blue lips, I hear a knock on the door. Frantically I wipe it off with tissues before my mom practically breaks down the door. She already knows what's up. I'm busted.

"What are you doing?"

"Why are you in my makeup?"

"You stay out of my makeup, you . . ."

" . . . you . . . "

"PERVERT!"

Atom bomb explosion.

I still remember her saying that, and for the longest time that scene will haunt me.

Thus starts the endless cycle of binging and purging. Times when I would still want to dress as a girl, coupled with times of sheer terror and trying to tell myself that I need to be more masculine.

## WANTING TO BE A GIRL

I guess that was the time my mom felt I needed to do more masculine things, and the only masculine thing I could do in my spare time (aside from playing with friends) was the Tiger Cub Scouts. So I joined Tiger Cubs. Had a good time, too. That led to Cub Scouts and then on to Boy Scouts. I recall one summer early into my Boy Scout days where everyone wanted to play *Star Wars*. Ok, it was *Return of the Jedi* technically but you get the drift. I could not figure out for the life of me why I was being made fun of because I wanted to play

# HOMOSEXUALITY

Princess Leia. Come on! I so wanted to be her. The hair, the soft skin, the makeup, the whole essence of being a woman, the outfit (the kick-ass attitude), everything. I wanted that. All of that. So why were people laughing at me? Oh right . . . I'm supposed to want to be Luke Skywalker or Han Solo. Uh huh.

Sooo . . . back to the binging and purging! Some how I managed to survive the years just doing whatever I could to feel somewhat female, yet be able to hide my tracks when I had to. I got really good at that.

In 1989 we moved to St. Petersburg, Florida. Fortunately for me, this still provided opportunity to dress whenever I could. In fact I would do it more. No one was home when I got home from school, so I had from 2:30–5 P.M. to be a girl. Okay, allow 30 minutes to clean and straighten up. 2:30–4:30 P.M. Monday through Friday. All year. Heaven. Plus when we moved, my sister and I had to share a room so not only did I have my mother's items available, I had my sister's clothing as well. And she was 8 years older so her clothes were much more hip than mom's. I started to experiment with different ways to create breasts. Including using water. First zip-lock bags until I realized they can leak. Then it was balloons. Balloons were good. They naturally formed a round shape. Perfect. Then I tried to tape them to me in an effort to create breasts. A lot of electrical tape (all I had available). I did have a boob break on me. That's not fun. Especially when you're using borrowed clothes. In an effort to cover my tracks I did the only logical thing I knew to get rid of them . . . flush 'em down the toilet. Which would have been fine and I would have gotten away with it if the toilet didn't clog on me. So with my mom screaming at me about my so-called intestinal problems, I had to get the maintanance man to come by and use this big metal hose thing to push whatever was clogged through the drains to clear the toilet line. Not fun. Humiliating beyond belief. So I purged. Again.

Later that year I got good at secretly moving some of my mom's lesser worn items to my dresser and hiding them under my jeans. So now, when everyone was asleep, I could be a girl. Heaven. Or so I thought.

One day my mom started screaming at me about how messy my dresser drawers were and how I need to dump them all out and fold and straighten everything and put it all back neatly. She almost opened the drawer where I was hiding my stash. I somehow convinced her that I would be a good kid and do that so she could get

## SELF-ACCEPTANCE AND IDENTITY

back to what she was doing. I was almost caught. Again. Fear racing through me, I realized I have to get better at being stealth.

Later that year (again) I was lying in bed. Dressed. And my mom walks in! I only panic on the inside. She comes up to the bed and tells me that she never did get to spend much time with me today. I assure her it's ok and I'm getting tired. She starts playing with my hair a little and she moves the covers down a bit and sees the strap of the undergarment I was wearing. Her only words: "Take that off."

She leaves the room so I can undress and I hand it to her, ashamed. I somehow go to sleep that night wondering what is going to happen to me in the morning.

Morning comes and my mom starts interrogating me about last night. One question that stands out in my mind was, "Do you touch yourself while wearing these clothes?" "No. eww, that's gross, no I don't do that!" Honestly, I didn't. I still hated "it." But now she thinks "it" caused this. Thanks a lot. She also asked why I did this. I had to come up with something, so I just blurted out "because I was bored." Thinking back, I don't know why I said that; it sounded good at the time.

And now, for three days out of the week I am in therapy. For something I didn't think was abnormal. At this point in my life, I learned how to lie really well. With a straight face, no less. Read on and you'll see . . .

## THERAPY

Therapist #1 was a tall older man. Looked like Lurch from the *Addams Family*, but better educated. I told him my story. I had a psych evaluation done. But for some reason he really wanted to focus on my relationship with my father. Never fully understood that. I guess my mom didn't either because we stopped going there. It was that or because I uttered the phrase, "I understand this was just a phase and I'm not going to do this again."

Therapist #2 I don't really remember. A younger guy. I think I was there for a whole 2 sessions. Again I uttered those magical words, and everything was fine.

Therapist #3 was a family counselor. This one was a nice middle-aged lady. Yeah, same old deal. I told her my story. Told her everything that happened up until that point and waited to see her reaction. So we talked for a while. I was getting ready to dish out my usual spiel until she caught me off guard. She was okay with it. Wait

. . . you mean it's okay for me to be this way? You're kidding. You want to actually HELP me be what I felt I should be? You totally rock, lady! She had me write down my plan and what I wanted to do and how I saw myself ten years down the road. Totally caught me off guard. Apparently it caught my mom off guard too because I wasn't there very long. Damn, and just when we were making progress!

So all that happened from 1989 to 1993. Fun times. More fun times ahead.

## EXPERIMENTING

In skewed logic, I figured since I want to be a girl, that I must be gay. I had heard about gay people before, didn't know any. So I experimented. Kind of. At first I got on-line with an adult BBS called "Variations" where I met a number of nice people of all walks of sexual preferences. That was where I met most of the people I had sex with. This was 1994 to 1995. . . . My mom eventually found out what I was up to (late night BBSing) and yanked the modem out of my computer. And my parents started tracking what I [did] and where I [went]. . . . I was on strict supervision. This was also the time [when] my mom, who I swear must be sadistic, started clipping out the obituaries of gay men who had died of AIDS and slipped them under my door for me to read. Every day I would have one. That was when I realized my mom was crazy. They didn't kick me out or disown me, though. That I am surprised at. But I was basically under house arrest.

Until I moved out! I was 21 and decided to move away to college and finish up my last two years. I had a dorm to myself and I was loving it! I even had [money] to spend. So like any true girl, I went shopping! Mostly for music, but I did buy a cute pair of bra and panties at K-Mart. Oh yeah, I'm living in Tampa now. So I got to dress every day. Whenever I wanted. As long as I wanted. I finally got to be a girl.

And along with a number of girls, I was raped in college. The guy knew about me, and felt obligated to enact the rape fantasy that supposedly all women have, but never act on. I don't remember if I went to my classes the next day, but I do remember crying myself to sleep that night and wanting to just throw out any girl clothes and to never want to dress again. I seriously kept to myself for the remainder of the year and eventually the guy left the college.

I also attended a few gay and lesbian coalition meetings at USF-Tampa. But I didn't feel I fit in so I stopped going. Plus their sched-

## SELF-ACCEPTANCE AND IDENTITY

ule was right during when I had classes.

In my senior year I met a girl. I won't cover up names. Her name was Jennifer. Things went well between us until I told her about my deep dark secret. She told me that she would leave me if I ever wanted to become a woman. It's not normal. You're a guy, act like it. I lied to myself and her for over 2 years. Finally I had enough of her and instead of her leaving me, I left her. Yeah, I'm a jerk, but in my eyes, it was do or die. Sink or swim. And I wasn't about to drown. She called me every name in the book and said how I was a loser and wouldn't amount to anything, that I'm sick in the head and a pervert and will always be. Finally I gave her a bold and confident "f— you" and hung up the phone. I treated my then good friend to pizza after that.

I learned that my friends would be the most important feature to my therapy and self-acceptance. They always have, and always will be.

I still continued to purge off and on. Until some time in the year 2000 after my last purge. Days after a purge I get strong urges to dress again and then get depressed when I have no outlet to do so. Or if I haven't dressed in awhile I will panic and only think about dressing and the need to be female. I almost failed a college final exam because of that. In a course on human sexuality. Ironic? I thought so.

## ENDING THE LIE

So year 2000 was the year I decided I would finally stop lying to myself. No more purges. I will start the road to self-acceptance and embrace who I am and what I want to be. That year my all around health increased exponentially.

Unfortunatly my parents weren't keen on my plans and tried to guilt trip me into being macho again. But, since they lived 30 minutes away, they couldn't do much. And I promised myself I wouldn't lie about this anymore, and I stuck to that promise.

Fast forward a few more years.

I am not full-time yet. I am part-time. I never thought I would get to this point. Ever. It's like a dream come true. I am in therapy. I am close to starting hormones [part of the sex-change process]. And I am much more confident in myself than I ever was before. I am finally out to almost everyone. My family knows, and although they aren't comfortable with it, they at least know the truth and aren't in denial about it. I'm sure my mom has lingering denial, but I have learned that I cannot make people accept me, they must do it themselves. I also learned that I must accept that I can only do so much and if someone has a problem with me, it is their problem and not mine, and I do not need to try and fix someone else's problem. That's been a big step for me.

I go out more now than I ever did. I pass [for female] 90% of the time and if anyone has an issue, they haven't brought it to my attention. I haven't had any violent issues to deal with. Some finger pointing but that's about it. So I have been very lucky so far. I currently have a girlfriend/fiancee who is very accepting of who I am and what I want to be. She helps me with everything. From fashion advice to makeup. She has been the most help in regards to how I present and carry myself, and in the mannerisms department. I found out it's the little things that can make or break your ability to pass. I think I have a lot of these down now.

# HALLOWEEN 2003

Wow . . . I have had the most interesting Halloween day today.

First, I went to work today as Alison. And as soon as I walked in to work and got up on the floor you could hear the jaws of people hitting the floor. Not only did their jaws hit the floor but they wouldn't stop staring! One could say that (tosses hair) yes I am that beautiful and stunning. But I know that they probably didn't expect me of all people to come in dressed as a girl, and I guess a convincing girl at that. I got a lot of compliments today, from my hair, to my nails, to my makeup, to general compliments on how I looked, or how pretty/cute/beautiful I looked. I got a lot of compliments. I ended up doing a lot of smiling and waving to people when they first walked in. I guess that's all you can do when someone is just staring at you like they've seen a ghost. . . .

I also got some flirty compliments today. A few guys trying to hit on me. My response to that was, "Honey, I am more woman than you can handle!" (little diva finger snap). They were playing with me, I thought to be playful too. Had one guy tell me twice, "Looking good there!" Tranny chasers at work . . . oy vey!!

I also managed to scare the entire "Commercial" department simply by saying that this isn't drag for me, it's normal, it's how I usually am. Yeah . . . they all just sat back down in their cubicles. . . .

But once people got over the initial shock, the response was 99.99% positive. So that is definitely cool. (big grin) And that's where I am at right now.

# Living with HIV: A Battle to Stay Alive

by David Morris

In the 1980s, when the human immunodeficiency virus (HIV) and its more deadly counterpart, acquired immune deficiency syndrome (AIDS), first surfaced among New York's homosexual population, the virus and disease were unjustly termed the "gay cancer" by those who believed it was some form of punishment reserved for gay men. Doctors knew little of the ailment in those early years, but they soon found that AIDS traveled freely into other populations as well. Intravenous drug users, prostitutes, and anyone engaging in unprotected sex were at risk for contracting the virus. This revelation did not lessen the burden on the gay community, though, which seemed to be hit hardest by HIV and AIDS. Before the disease was fully understood and drugs could be developed to combat the debilitating effects, AIDS killed thousands of homosexuals while HIV impaired the freedom and strength of thousands more.

David Morris was diagnosed with HIV in 1984 and has lived with it since. In the following narrative, Morris explains how he has yet avoided acquiring full-blown AIDS through a combination of luck and a regimen of medications. In the late 1980s, Morris participated in many clinical trials for new drugs that could stave off AIDS and return some measure of his health. In 1995, after developing Hodgkin's lymphoma as a result of the virus, he underwent chemotherapy to battle that cancer. When the lymphoma went into remission, he went back to his battery of antiviral drugs. All of this treatment has left him physically weakened but mentally unbowed. Now at age fifty he continues to struggle against the disease while offering his support to others who are suffering from it. He currently serves as an administrator of the wellness program at Beth Israel Deaconess Medical Center in Boston.

David Morris, "Living with HIV—A Survivor's Perspective," *Positively Aware*, November/December 2001. Copyright © 2001 by Test Positive Aware Network. Reproduced by permission.

My AIDS drugs make me sick, but I take them anyway. It would be great to take a "drug holiday," but I don't dare because I don't want my viral loads to skyrocket and I don't want my virus to become resistant to my medications.

Sometimes I get tired of taking my medications, which are little daily reminders that I have a disease for which there is no cure. I miss not being able to drink my morning coffee until I've eaten my breakfast and taken my pills. I miss the freedom of being able to come and go as I please without worrying when and where I'll take my medications. But HIV doesn't take a holiday, so neither do I. It's difficult, but it's worth it, because I've seen what can happen when HIV-positive people don't take their medications [or don't have access to medications].

My 20s and 30s weren't as carefree as I thought they would be. I suffered while I watched the deaths of more than 50 friends from a mysterious disease that was then called "gay cancer" or gay-related immune deficiency (GRID). I saw them go blind. I saw their bodies covered in lesions caused by the AIDS-related cancer Kaposi's sarcoma. I saw them die horrible deaths, with no medications to help ease their pain.

When I was diagnosed in 1984, I was scared. Although I had witnessed the power of HIV first hand, I suffered in silence for the first year. I was afraid of letting the world know my status, afraid my co-workers would shun me, and afraid that my medical insurance would drop me.

When I finally got the courage to seek treatment, I had to battle the ignorance and prejudices of the times. In the early days of the virus, there were physicians who were just as afraid of AIDS as the general public. In 1985, I at last found a physician who was familiar with infectious diseases, one who understood my disease and my desire to fight it. That physician prepared me to battle HIV.

## PARTICIPATING IN CLINICAL TRIALS

Later that year, I agreed to participate in a clinical trial of AZT (zidovudine), the first antiretroviral medication. For nine months I took 1,200mg of AZT every day, which was the dosage approved by the FDA [Food and Drug Administration] in 1987. The side effects were awful. My ears rung, my joints ached, I felt anxious, nauseated and like I was in a fog, but I stuck with it because I knew death was the alternative. I wasn't ready to die.

It was the experience of patients like myself who eventually gave doctors and researchers the clinical information they needed to determine that the appropriate dose of AZT is 600mg daily [approved by the FDA in 1990]. I continued on AZT and participated in other clinical trials. I did what I could to keep my viral load down to prolong my life.

## CANCER SCARE

In May 1995, I was diagnosed with Hodgkin's lymphoma and had to discontinue all of my antiretroviral medications. I underwent months of chemotherapy that left me feeling like I was living in a dead man's body. However, after nearly two years, my cancer went into remission.

I immediately resumed my fight against HIV. After so long without my antiretroviral medications, my T-cells had dropped drastically. In 1997, I resumed the antiretroviral medication that had been working for me before my cancer diagnosis. But, this time, my viral load continued to rise and my T-cells continued to drop. My virus had mutated and become resistant to the drugs. I had to switch medications.

In 1998, I started a new, triple-drug therapy and I've been on this regimen ever since. I take my medications three times a day, seven pills a day, seven days a week. It's not easy, because the side effects can be debilitating and the pills are a constant reminder that I have HIV. But I know that I must take my pills every day for the rest of my life, no matter what. I know firsthand what it means to have "AIDS battle fatigue," but I continue to take my pills because I'm not ready to give up. I want to stay alive.

## LIVING WITH THE SIDE EFFECTS

My medications cause myopathy, which makes my muscles ache, and neuropathy, which affects my nerves so that sometimes I can't feel my feet when I walk, and my fingers and toes tingle. I've been in pain for the past couple months, but I've found ways to ease it with pain medications, acupuncture and regular exercise.

I'm willing to deal with my side effects for now because my medications are working, but there are days when the battle fatigue is so strong I don't want to take another pill. What keeps me going is knowing that being 100 percent adherent to my medications gives me the best chance of living longer with HIV.

The mental strength to stick with my drug regimen comes from the memories of what I witnessed in the early days of HIV and AIDS. I saw the virus devastate the lives of my friends and my community. I was around when physicians and scientists were frantically looking for something, anything that could help the people who were dying. When antiretrovirals were created, I jumped at the chance to take them. I haven't looked back and I've never missed a dose.

To make sure, I put my medications in pillboxes designed to hold all the pills I need for seven days. I fill these pillboxes once a month so I can have them when I need them. I keep a pillbox next to my bathrobe so that every day when I wake up, I see them and remember what I have to do.

## EMBRACING MY HIV STATUS

Despite the side effects and the schedule for my medications, I try to live as normal a life as possible. I can't afford to get sick again, because I've got to spread the word about HIV at schools and to anybody who will listen. There's not much publicity about the disease these days—no nightly stories on the news about young men and women who have died a ghastly death from AIDS. People need to be reminded that people still die from AIDS. Today, some young people think HIV is not such a big deal, kind of like high blood pressure—something you can control and still lead a "normal" life. It's as important as ever to prevent infection with HIV.

For people living with HIV, it's important that they know HIV can be treated. HIV-positive people must stop feeling guilty about contracting HIV and seek medical help, including one-on-one counseling to help adjust to a new life. HIV is a tough disease with a lot of rules, but if someone decides to begin antiretroviral medications, then drug adherence is one rule that must be obeyed.

Once HIV-positive people accept their status, I believe it's important to become involved in support groups. Support groups provide a safe place for us to express ourselves, gain insights from people who are dealing with the same issues, and remember we are not alone. It has helped me to become involved in helping others with HIV and it reminds me that my life is important and has a purpose. I serve on the board of directors of two AIDS service organizations in Boston, and participate in many AIDS education programs. I feel good knowing that I'm helping others.

When people are diagnosed with HIV, they have two choices: fight or give in. I chose to fight and I've never regretted it.

# CHAPTER 4

*Discrimination*

SOCIAL ISSUES FIRSTHAND

# Negative Attitudes Toward Homosexuality Have Not Changed

by Youth Panel Participants

In January 2002, the Media Project, a Los Angeles–based sexual health advocacy organization, held a panel discussion on images of homosexuality in popular television programs. Part of the conversation contended with whether the increased number of gay characters in media programming was leading to greater acceptance of the gay community in America. The panel, which was composed primarily of gay and lesbian teens and young people from the Los Angeles area, acknowledged that representing homosexuals on television was a welcome change. However, they argued that the gay characters portrayed were often too exaggerated and one-dimensional. By relating some recent experiences from their own lives, the youth panel participants maintained that homophobia still dominates the mindset of people whom they come in contact with every day—from classmates to parents to health care professionals.

The Media Project works with the entertainment industry to ensure that responsible sexual health information and images are being broadcast on television. The moderator of this panel was Wilson Cruz, a young gay actor who came to national attention for playing an openly gay character on the teen television drama *My So-Called Life*. Also in attendance was Gwenn Baldwin, the executive director of the Los Angeles Gay and Lesbian Center.

*Wilson Cruz, Moderator:* First let me say how proud I am to be here. We are here to inspire you to tell better stories, truthful stories about GLBT [gay, lesbian, bisexual, transgender] youth. A lot of us thought that with the start of a new millennium, attitudes towards gays would be much further along. And although it is getting better, we still experience much discrimination and fear. Let us be-

Robin Smalley, "Growing Up Gay: Inside Out in America," www.themediaproject.com, January 30, 2002. Copyright © 2002 by The Media Project. Reproduced by permission.

gin with how you feel about attitudes towards gays and if you think things have changed?

*Jessie G:* Personally, I have had the most difficulties regarding my appearance. People constantly think I'm a man based on the way I look and present myself, even though I am a woman. I will relate this story to you that happened to me yesterday at the airport. Since security has been heightened at the airports, they randomly select people to "pat down" and search. I was chosen to be searched and was sent to the male security person who patted me down. They thought that I was a man. That happens to me a lot. Every day I have to put on a tough face.

*Luis:* I went to an all Latino East LA high school and came out at 15. I went through so much shame. It was hard for my family. My father and mother had a very hard time and they are just now understanding who I am. My parents thought that all gay men would be hair dressers. I always liked guy stuff. I want people to know me for myself and not because I am gay. Being gay is such a small portion of my life.

*Jessie F:* I went to a Catholic school and had to change schools two other times because of gay discrimination by students, teachers and principals. I was very sheltered when I was growing up and I didn't grow up with any queer people. My conflict with my religion has been very hard for me. My parents separated me from my two sisters because they thought my sisters would "catch" being gay from me. I was very suicidal and wanted to run away. I thought I would go to hell for being gay or just die. I have been beat up in the school bathroom. You have to be very careful in the work world. You must decide what you can and can't present about yourself to your work.

## ENTRENCHED CULTURAL STIGMAS

*Luis:* I would like for us to touch upon the aspect of how your religious and cultural beliefs fit into being gay. I know that first you have to deal with just being gay. I lived in a small community. I knew I felt different but I didn't know why or what it was. The Latino culture does not accept being gay. I am Catholic and they would tell me that being gay is wrong. That filled me with self hate. My parents thought tough love was the way to go. I would always hear the words "coto" or "maricon" which are Hispanic words, bad words, meaning something like faggot.

*Wilson:* Yes I remember always hearing the word "maricon." It is such a bad word. How is it different for a Latino, or an Asian or a religious person, etc. "to come out?"

*Luis:* I wasn't exposed to many things. I felt different but I didn't know why. To be gay in my culture is not accepted . . . thinking you are gay was such a curse. I felt why was this happening to me? Nobody was saying or is saying it's ok, they say it is wrong.

*Wilson:* I used to go to mass with my mother. The priest didn't know how to say "gay" in Spanish. For two hours I heard the word "maricon." I never went back.

*Bev:* We are 49 different countries, China, Cambodia, Filipinos, Vietnam, etc. I come from a less conservative family. Being in the US made it easier for myself. When I came out my mom was giving me messages, the paternal views: women take care of the house and men will take care of women, monetarily; she was worried who was going to support me? I said to her I was going to support *myself* and my partner.

*Wilson:* You are dealing with sexuality and also with gender roles. It's not just sexual orientation. How do you feel when in this American society women can support themselves but then go back home and hear that it is the role of man to support woman?

*Lexi:* I went to Beverly Hills High School. It was like going with the cast of 90210. It was a very difficult time. At school there was a gay-straight alliance but still we had problems. I had so much internal homophobia and I also was very promiscuous. I always heard the word gay and lesbian in a negative context. I had attempted suicide and went to a mental institution. I get upset when everyone thinks my life was perfect.

*Anthony:* I came out at 14. My mother cried every day for a month and my dad was passive aggressive. He just moped around. He tried to ignore my comments but sometimes he talked back. In high school I heard rude comments. My tactic was to ignore them. When I said something they often stopped right there . . . quite odd. . . .

## IGNORANCE IN THE MEDICAL COMMUNITY

*Wilson:* How is this stigmatized in the medical community?

*Gwenn Baldwin:* It definitely has an impact.

*Wilson:* Obviously this may lead to some higher rates of risky behavior: tell us how.

*Gwenn:* Obviously information is knowledge and if you are in-

## DISCRIMINATION

formed and aware of how you can protect your health, you will be better off. . . . But I think the major impact from discrimination from the health care universe is the lack of appropriate health care. Thus the risky behaviors, if you are not getting the health care and you are getting only a small portion of it, your health is going to be jeopardized, and I think that that is the largest issue. And on top of that again is your feelings of self worth, and your ability to take charge of your life can be greatly diminished, and that has an impact because what do you do if you are in pain? You medicate. Substance abuse is a serious issue. Alcohol and drug abuse have higher rates of use in LGBT kid communities than they do on the streets. They medicate. And that actually is what leads to risky behavior more than anything else does, not the specific lack of information around. If you are on crystal meth or on ecstasy or any number of drugs, your inhibitions are way down, your need to be connecting with people and to be reinforced in any positive way and at times your positive is, you know, a sexual encounter. Yes that is where the problem lies. . . .

*Wilson:* And can any of you share your experiences with receiving medical attention, medical care? I was told that, Jessie, you might have some experiences.

*Jessie G:* Well, I mean, I think the first time I went to the gynecologist, I felt the same insecurities that were exactly what Gwenn said. First, I was asked if I was sexually active and I said, "Yes." Then she asked, "Do you use condoms," and I said, "No." Then when I said I have sex with women, the doctor walked out. And she walked out, and she stayed out for about 20 minutes. And you know that doctors are kind of bad about that anyway, but she didn't even say anything, she just walked out. And you know that to this day I feel like it's ridiculous, 'cause I'm the medical health educator in my profession now. Actually I had to go to the gynecologist yesterday, and I had to tell the person what sort of services I need. I had to educate the person. And if I'm a 23- or 24-year-old that has to do that, because I am empowered with all this information, that's great. If I was a 16-year-old that went in, or an 18-year-old and not had this information, because I didn't have resources that were taught to me in my sexual health class in my school, I would not have been able to take care of myself. I would not have been able to say, "Yes, I need these tests. Yes, I need that information." I think that it's important and it's exhausting trying to, you know, teach your doctor who has gone to school for 7 years that you need these tests. They should do the work for you, right?

## YOU DON'T IDENTIFY ANYWHERE

*Lexi:* It's really hard, like I know when I started coming out, I stopped watching TV because seeing all these stereotypes out there, it's probably not what you want to hear, but seeing all these stereotypes out there, and you are trying to find your place in the queer community. It's very complicated. And that is why we are here today and that's why we are meeting with you. It's very, very hard because these shows only have one character. And when they do, they're very stereotypical or very anti-stereotypical but there are so many different facets of being a queer youth and to try to identify tends to be very difficult. And not only now are you not feeling that you identify with the straight community, you don't feel like you identify with the queer community that you are seeing on TV. And then you don't identify anywhere, and you are a complete outcast, and it's the end of the world.

# Black and Gay: Facing Racism and Homophobia

by Ed Brock

Maintaining an identity as a homosexual in a society that is predominantly heterosexual is a challenge faced by almost every gay person. Whether a person is openly gay or still "in the closet" matters little; for he or she is ultimately confronted by homophobic attitudes and negative stereotyping of their chosen sexual orientation. To be gay means being alienated and demoted to a minority status in nearly every culture throughout the world.

The difficulty of such a situation is compounded when a person is not only gay, but also a member of a racial minority. Ed Brock, a secondary school history teacher in the Bronx, is an openly gay African American. A self-proclaimed activist and "outed" homosexual since his college days, Brock has served on the steering committee for the New York Metro chapter of the Gay, Lesbian, and Straight Education Network.

In the following narrative, Brock discusses coming to terms with his identity both as a black youth and a burgeoning homosexual. He says, both of these facets of his identity forced him to learn harsh lessons while navigating adolescence. In his estimation, learning to be black meant learning to be silent, and learning to be gay meant having to pretend to be something else in order to achieve acceptance.

The lessons Brock learned early on were carried forth, subconsciously, into his professional career as a teacher. Ed details the moment when he recognized how the years of silence and pretending had affected the way he taught his own students. As a result, he came out to the faculty and student body of the school where he worked. This act was liberating, but Brock acknowledges that the discrimination he faced while growing into manhood has made being silent and pretending into unhealthy "habits" that he is still trying to overcome.

Ed Brock, "Coons and Corpses: A Lesson Unlearned," *Telling Tales Out of School: Gays, Lesbians, and Bisexuals Revisit Their School Days,* edited by Kevin Jennings. Los Angeles: Alyson Publications, 1998. Copyright © 1998 by Ed Brock. Reproduced by permission.

## HOMOSEXUALITY

I can't believe I just impulsively spent close to 30 bucks on books. Fag books. Thirty bucks on fag stories. Thirty bucks!!!

Not that reading gay fiction is a sin—at least not in my book. And not that it isn't OK to treat myself every now and then to a book that I can read simply for pleasure (and they *were* for pleasure). I bought *Captain Swing* by Larry Duplechan and *Going To Meet The Man* and *Just Above My Head*—the *original* black gay novel, thank you very much—by James Baldwin. I guess I'm on one of my *let-me-rediscover-the-black-gay-brilliance-of-Brother-James* kicks again, because yesterday I also bought a copy of *Another Country*, in addition to buying the *Men on Men 6* collection of contemporary (white) gay fiction, edited by David Bergman.

No, reading gay fiction ain't a sin. But my consumption of gay literature seems to come in binges. Like the bulimic who gorges on bon-bons in a moment of weakness, I splurge on books—gay books—when my self-esteem needs a boost. Just like I waste money and time enduring gay dance clubs and cruising guys on the A train when I need that boost. Or just like I get catty and trifling with other desperate-for-attention queens on Christopher Street, spend hours surfing the Net for anything gay-related, and desperately make my rounds at bourgie gay support groups, looking for that boost. All of this because at 23—after going to college and coming out and being a fierce black queer activist and scholar and graduating from college and getting a job and getting my own apartment in New York City and hearing people tell me that I'm *making it*—I'm still hopelessly and aimlessly looking for affirmation. I'm still looking for my damn f—ing reflection.

## THE FIRST TIME I REALIZED I WAS DIFFERENT

Lesson #1: I remember when they beat me up in fifth grade. It was during recess, right after an intense soccer game between the kids from my homeroom teacher's class and the kids from Ms. Clark's homeroom class. I forget the exact reason why they beat me up. But I do remember that for several weeks prior, this white kid named Christian had insisted on repeatedly sharing his discovery of the word "nigger" with our classmates. I remember being jumped toward the far end of the soccer field by Christian and two or three other white boys as they called me "nigger" and beat me like I was one. I remember other kids—most of them white—passively watching, some of them confused, some of them entertained. I remember eventually breaking away and running inside, where Ms. Clark noticed my shaken demeanor, my grass-stained shirt, and my unrelenting tears. And I remember not telling Ms. Clark the reason why I was upset, for even back then I seemed to know that I wasn't supposed to speak up when white people used their power to hurt me. This marked the first time I could remember being aware, being overwhelmed, by the fact that I was different. And this marked the first time I could remember ever getting a lesson in how to be silent.

Why the hell am I writing in fragments? Why can't I just script a cute and quick essay on how it felt to a be a closeted queer in junior and senior high school? High School?! . . . , do I even remember what it was like to be a closeted black queer in high school? As soon as I graduated, I ran away, far away, and never looked back. I went to college, I came out, and I conquered the world, or at least the . . . campus. Protected by the PC liberalism of an early '90s college campus, I erased the traumatic episodes of my high school career from my memory. Nobody wants to remember life in the closet after coming out. So now there are gaps in my memory and gaps in my story. My story resists being neatly compressed into a fluid, *Stand-By-Me*-style, coming-of-age narrative. While all of the excerpts in this piece are related to one another, fitting them into a narrative is impossible. Using them to formulate a fluid narrative would allow me to understand my story, and more dangerously, to control it. Clearly, the forces-that-be do not intend for me to control my narrative. They are too afraid of what I would learn if I could put all of the pieces neatly together. And quite honestly, I think that I, too, am afraid of what my narrative, in order and intact, would reveal.

## LEARNING TO PRETEND IN ORDER TO BE ACCEPTED

Lesson #2: Fifth grade was an important year for me. I discovered some crucial facts of life. One discovery came right before Christmas, when I played Ebenezer Scrooge in the fifth-grade production of *A Christmas Carol*. There I was, this cute little black boy in a predominantly middle-class white suburban public school, with the lead role in the school play. *How the hell did this little Negro get the lead part?* is what my father expected the white folks in the audience to say, or at least to think. Over weeks of memorizing lines, getting fitted for fab! costumes, and keeping my patience through long and tiring rehearsals, I feared that the audience wouldn't like me. I was worried, frightened. But you know what? When the curtains opened, Ms. Thing stepped on stage and turned that role out. I sang, I screamed, I pranced up and down that stage like an overanxious diva on Broadway. Basically, I worked (SNAP!). And the crowd loved me. They loved *me*. The well-dressed, well-paid white parents loved *me*. They smiled at me and praised me. My teachers showered me with adulation. Even my peers congratulated me (and, much to the heart's content of this diva-in-the-making, *envied* me). I enjoyed the applause, and I learned a valuable lesson. I learned that I could win people's affection when I pretended to be someone, or something, else. I learned that people enjoyed me when I was on stage; I learned that people approved of me when I pretended to be someone, or something, that I was not. When I pretended to be someone, or something, that they wanted to see. Of all the things that I was taught in grade school, this was one of the few lessons that I truly understood—that I truly learned.

## EARLY IMAGES OF BLACK HOMOSEXUALS

There weren't many images of black gay men circulating through popular media when I was in high school in the late '80s. Well, at least I didn't have access to many images. In fact, only two images come to mind: the flaming snap queens Antoine and Blaine on the TV show *In Living Color*, and the pictures of the men who were killed and devoured by Jeffrey Dahmer. As I struggled to construct a sense of self as a closeted black gay teenager, the only images I saw of other black gay men were the buffoonish derisions of Negro faggotry offered by homophobic black male comics and the hazy snapshots of the victims of a cannibalistic white gay psychopath. I remember the condescending laughter directed at those limp-wristed parodies of black sissies; I remember aunts and old black church ladies looking at newspaper pictures of Dahmer's victims, quoting verses from Leviticus and Romans, and declaring smugly, "That's what happens when you live *that* life of sin."

These were the contexts in which I received images of black gay men when I was in high school. During those ever so formative years, with no other resources at my disposal, I searched for my reflection in coons and corpses. When watching *In Living Color*, I scavenged for redeeming qualities in being oversexed and misogynist. I derived pleasure from saying "Hated it" every time Blaine and Antoine reviewed a movie starring women; I misconstrued their exaggerated appetite for male chests, cocks, and ass as an act of black gay sexual liberation. And while looking at the pictures of Dahmer's victims, I explored their eyes, their lips, and their smiles. I searched for indications of buffed black bodies, and I imagined them as my lovers, engaged in my embrace. I did all of this because coons and corpses were the only images of black gay men that I saw, and I mistook them for my reflection. . . .

## HUMILIATION IN HIGH SCHOOL

Lesson #3: I know there is a God because it was God who prevented me from stabbing Damon, Chris, Shane, and Jay in the tenth grade. This was the clique of macho-acting boys who played on the football team, bragged about the sex and the drugs that they really hadn't had, and asserted their fragile masculinity by harassing me, the class sissy, on a daily basis throughout the tenth grade. They mocked my effeminate manner and taunted me with epithets. They wrote ED IS A FAG on the walls of the boys' bathrooms. In gym class they ridiculed my lack of athletic prowess. In health class they brought attention to the fact that I surrounded myself with platonic female friends with whom I gossiped and even went shopping; they accused me of being one of the girls. And often they did these things in front of girls, as a way to advertise their virility to potential female lovers.

I realize that I was lucky—they never hit me. They never hit me, however, because I never talked back. I always took these verbal beatings silently, afraid of the physical beatings that would occur if I were to speak up. My silence bred terror. I was terrified every time I had to endure their barrage of accusations. I died every time they brought my unannounced, but widely suspected, faggotry to everyone's attention. I felt powerless as they stripped my sexual identity on the auction block for public inspection. This sense of powerlessness in the company of my peers became the lens through which I learned to despise and hate myself—a lesson which Damon, Chris, Shane, and Jay taught me on a daily basis. I didn't speak up, not only because I was afraid of physical retaliation, but also because I didn't believe that I was worth speaking up for. They knew, our other classmates knew, and tragically, I knew that black faggots were pathetic, sick, worthless. I had no place, no right, to challenge such a commonly accepted truth.

Yet at the same time that I felt terrified, powerless, and worthless, I was also consumed with rage. Every time Damon, Chris, Shane, and Jay harassed me, a bloodthirsty rage threatened to occlude my air flow, cut off my circulation, trouble my bowels. At night, in the privacy of my own room, while still awake, I would fantasize about violent episodes in health class where I would wield ice picks, trash cans, metal pipes, and daggers to mutilate my four foes. . . . Then one morning, having been pushed to the edge with rage, I took my mother's 9-inch butcher's knife from the kitchen, placed it in my duffel bag, and got on the school bus. I had come to a decision: *If they f—— with me today, I'll stab them.* Never mind the fact that I would have gone to jail, that my life would have been ruined—another young black brother lost. No, they had pushed me to the edge, and their time to pay had come.

But as I said, I know that there's a God because God prevented me from stabbing Damon, Chris, Shane, and Jay that day in the tenth grade. Instead of going to health class, I was called to the guidance office to see my counselor—for what I cannot remember. All I know is that missing health class that day gave me an opportunity to catch my cool. It gave me an opportunity to rediscover my terror, my fear, and my disgust for myself. It gave me an opportunity to remember that I had no place, no right, to challenge Damon, Chris, Shane, and Jay. I've heard many stories of queer youth inflicting violence on themselves or on others as a response to the homophobic [bulls—] they experience on a daily basis. But I rediscovered my hatred for myself before I got the chance to carry out such violence. I guess I was lucky.

## "WE TEACH WHO WE ARE"

"We teach who we are." Those were the words that accosted me on a late August afternoon at the George School, a private boarding school in eastern Pennsylvania. Just about two weeks before beginning my second year as a history teacher at an elite private school in New York City, I attended a series of workshops held at the George School for young teachers of color. One of the facilitators wrote this sentence on a piece of newsprint and proceeded to recognize how our demeanor, ideals, and character as teachers are the lessons that our students remember the most. In our students' eyes, names and dates of historical figures and events pale in comparison to how our own beliefs inform the ways in which we run our classrooms and interact with students. I immediately thought of my fourth grade teacher, Mrs. Sinters; the only thing I remember about my experience in her class is how she ignored and disempowered me and the handful of other black students in the class on a regular basis. She didn't care too much for black children, and she definitely taught who she was.

I sat in horror as my memory shifted from Mrs. Sinters's class to my own experiences as a first-year teacher. After being *very* out and *very* political in college, I had decided to revisit the closet during my first year as a teacher. With New York being one of the 40 states in which gay men and lesbians can be fired from their jobs because of their gayness, with the absence of "sexual orientation" from my school's antidiscrimination policy, and with the hysteria that erupts around the inclusion of gay issues in secondary education, I opted for closeted silence and a paycheck as a first-year teacher over job insecurity and political drama. Sure, the kids knew—I didn't fool anybody. Kids can put two and two together rather easily. But since I evaded their inquiries into my sexuality, they accepted me. They knew I was gay, and they knew I was going to be silent, so they accepted me.

And so I sat in horror that afternoon at the George School as I considered what I had taught my students during my first year of teaching. I thought that I had taught them about medieval European guilds, Spanish conquistadors, and the American Revolution. But what I had really taught them was that I was beat up by white boys in the fifth grade and learned how to be silent. What I had really taught them was that I was harassed on a daily basis in the tenth grade and learned how to hate myself. What I had really taught them was that as a black gay teenager in a predominantly middle-class white suburban high school, I learned, as Paul Lawrence Dunbar once wrote, to "wear the masks." I learned to wear the masks of docility, assimilation, fear, and silence.

## RACISM AND HOMOPHOBIA

These are the lessons that my students took with them, and these are the lessons that make growing up so difficult for gay and lesbian teenagers, especially gay and lesbian teens of color. For while all teenagers suffer whenever they are taught to be silent, gay and lesbian kids of color face a particular dilemma. It incenses me when I hear people of color express their homophobia by proclaiming that homophobia and racism are not alike, that racism is clearly the more horrific of the two, and that gay people have no right to make such a comparison. It incenses me because I can recall from my own experience that while being a black child in a racially conservative community was difficult, I at least had resources that I could turn to. I could go to my parents, black teachers (the few that there were), or other black adults in the community for guidance. I could sit down at the "black kids' table" in the cafeteria during lunch, or I could attend a meeting of my school's Black Student Union when I needed to vent. I could call upon local black churches and the local chapter of the NAACP [National Association for the Advancement of Colored People] when I needed community assistance. When I got beat up by white boys in the fifth grade; when my ninth-grade history teacher defended "the white man's burden" in class one day as a worthwhile doctrine; when skinheads appeared in my high school during my junior year; or when the Ku Klux Klan held a march in my hometown two days before Martin Luther King Jr.'s birthday during my senior year of high school, there was a community of black people to whom I could turn for support. This community protected me, nurtured me, and provided me with the tools that I needed to face a racist world.

No equivalent support systems were available to me as a gay student. There weren't any openly gay students in whom I could confide. There weren't any openly gay teachers or other adults who could counsel and guide me. I didn't have access to any larger gay community that could shelter me, nurture me, and teach me the skills that I needed to confront a homophobic world. While I gradually gained confidence in and love for my blackness, and as I gradually learned to celebrate and embrace it despite racism, my gayness remained suppressed and despised. So homophobic people of color do have a point: homophobia and racism are, in fact, different. For gay kids of color, however, the former is not necessarily the lesser of the two evils.

Regardless of how racism and homophobia are different, one important similarity remains: both teach silence and self-hatred. These were lessons that racism and homophobia taught me all too well, and these were lessons that I taught my students as a first-year teacher. . . .

## COMING OUT AS A TEACHER

Overall, coming out as a gay teacher was a positive event. Sure, there were those kids whose religious/moral beliefs, or whose immaturity and personal insecurities around sexuality, led them to make snide comments behind my back. But to my amazement, many students overwhelmed me in the halls with adulation and praise. . . . Why? Because all kids want to learn how to speak up, speak out, and affirm who they are. This was definitely what I longed for as a closeted, petrified, self-loathing black gay teenager; some things just haven't changed.

But after the initial rounds of adulation and praise, my glorious moment of self-affirmation was tempered by the cool realization that coming out never solves all of one's problems. After all, we live in the same homophobic and heterosexist society *after* coming out as we did beforehand. Quickly I noticed which students and teachers did *not* offer me encouragement and support; I became paranoid about how our relationships would change for the worse. Quickly (and I do mean *quickly*) I became annoyed by and suspicious of fellow faculty members who wanted to tell me stories about gay cousins and lesbian aunts, proving how "cool" they were with "the issue." I revisited my anxiety over the parental disdain, administrative panic, and job insecurity that might result from my actions. Gradually . . . I took a step back and surrendered my confidence to self-doubt, angst, and most of all, fear.

## IDENTITY IS A HARD HABIT TO BREAK

Ironically, in my attempt to unlearn the lessons of self-hatred and fear that I had internalized as a youth, I realized that these lessons, at least for me, will never be completely unlearned. Silence and self-doubt, for me, are like biting my fingernails and filing my income-tax at the last minute: habits I will constantly struggle to overcome. But I must say, for the time being, I'm comforted by the fact that after sorting through this messy warehouse of adolescent memories, for the first time in my life I finally realize what the struggle actually is. And with this knowledge, I can actually begin to fight.

# A Marine Officer Under "Don't Ask, Don't Tell"

by Luke, interviewed by Steven Zeeland

In an anthology of interviews conducted with U.S. Marines, Steven Zeeland focuses on the topic of homosexuality in the Marine Corps. In a 1994 interview excerpted below, Zeeland talks to Major Luke, a thirty-seven-year-old gay marine who was then stationed at Camp Pendleton near San Diego. Two years previously, when Bill Clinton had promised to improve the relations between gay military personnel and the armed services, Luke had written a letter to the new president showing his support and appreciation. After Clinton instituted the "don't ask, don't tell" policy, Luke felt betrayed. The policy forbids military recruiters from asking whether an applicant is a homosexual, but it allows the military to discharge gay service members who are open about their sexuality. Yet as this interview reveals, Luke is at least content being stationed on the West Coast where there are many opportunities to interact with the gay community in California.

Luke tells Zeeland that since he has come out as a gay marine, he feels better about himself, but he still does not broadcast his homosexuality because he is aware of the homophobic attitudes that seem ingrained in the U.S. military. Luke maintains that he is proud of being a marine, but he is also proud of being gay. While he must be on guard to keep the two aspects of his personality from coming into conflict, Luke asserts that if being gay gave the Marine Corps cause to discharge him, he would not suffer the humiliation quietly.

*Zeeland:* When we last spoke you'd written a letter to Bill Clinton expressing your hopes that he would live up to the expectations of you and the other people who elected him. How do you feel about President Clinton now?

*Luke:* Betrayed. I would have had a lot more respect for Clinton if he had done what he had promised and lost, than getting what he

Steven Zeeland, *The Masculine Marine: Homoeroticism in the U.S. Marine Corps.* Binghamton, NY: Harrington Park Press, 1996. Copyright © 1996 by The Haworth Press, Inc. All rights reserved. Reproduced by permission.

and [Congressman] Barney Frank and others say was a half-victory. There are people in the military who came out because they believed his promises. . . .

## WEST COAST MARINE

*Z:* You said that people have been telling you that you seem to be a happier person those days.

*L:* Yeah. My friend Tracy Thorne, he's told me on the phone that David Mixner says there's been a big change over me. And some other people, too, said I look a lot happier since I've been out here [in San Diego]. Which is probably true.

*Z:* You've just come back from North Carolina. I'm told there's a big difference between the East Coast Marine Corps and the West Coast Marine Corps. Do you think it's a lot harder for Marines to be gay in North and South Carolina than it is in Southern California?

*L:* It's different. Before I left, I was starting to meet a few gay enlisted Marines, and they had their own little community. They all went to the beach together, and they'd go out to what local bars there were. I'm sort of a big city person, so it was more frustrating for me; I wanted to participate in more urban gay community things. I wanted to join a gay running club, or a gay scuba diving club, or a gay hiking club. It's not that I feel that I have to be in gay organizations, but I wanted the option. And there were no options out there. There, instead of developing what you'd like to be, you have to accept what's available.

*Z:* Of course there are more above-ground gay meeting places here in San Diego, but another guy I interviewed who was leaving Camp Pendleton for Lejeune [a camp in North Carolina] thought that he might find more opportunities for sex there, in underground places that don't tend to exist as much here, where people are more likely to feel forced to either surface as "gay," or not do anything at all.

## OBJECTIFIED

*L:* There's a big difference between officers and enlisted. I don't live in a barracks. I don't hang around with a hundred and fifty other guys my age that I can explore possibilities with. I lived out in town, by myself. I worked with mostly other officers, who were all married and have families. As an officer, I was suspect among the enlisted, when I did run into enlisted people out in town, or in the one bar. Unless I was introduced by somebody else. And even when they knew who I was, I was still not let all the way in. When you did go out, half the crowd wanted to go to bed with you because you were an officer, and the other half wanted to stay away from you because you were an officer. There weren't a whole lot of people who wanted to know you as a person.

*Z:* How does it make you feel when people are sexually attracted to you as a Marine Corps officer?

*L:* It doesn't make me feel very good. I guess I can understand maybe some of what women complain about, in some ways. Anyone who wanted to be friends with me, I was immediately suspicious of their reasons. I actually stopped going out as much, because, if you did meet somebody, and if you did spend time with them, and afterwards you found out you were right, it was just a one-time notch-on-the-bedpost deal just because you were an officer—it didn't make me feel good.

*Z:* Did you feel objectified?

*L:* Yeah. I just . . . I'm an officer in the Marine Corps, and there is the pride, the respect, everything that comes with that. I do my job, and I'm very professional. But as a person, my picture of me is not as an officer in the Marine Corps. It's just like being gay: it's only a part of me, it's not the whole of me. And the problem is, going out some places, that's all you were. You were nothing else. I think it's kind of sad. Because you're a lot of things. You may be a philosopher, a lover, a good runner, great at handicrafts, or whatever. . . .

## ANALYZING ATTITUDES

*Z:* Since coming out, has your view of what is masculine become any less rigid?

*L:* I think I'm not as concerned about whether or not I'm portraying somebody else's view of masculinity. I'm no longer concerned about projecting a particular image. I'm not gonna deceive. I've even gone as far as—another officer who worked for me made some fairly stupid remarks about gays. In fact, we were out in the field, showering in a tent, and he started spouting off that this was one reason why he would never allow gays in the military, because he would never shower next to a homosexual. After mouthing under my breath, "Too late," I challenged him right there. I said, "Why does it matter to you?" "Huh?" "If you're comfortable in your own sexuality, what should it matter to you if you're showering next to

## DISCRIMINATION

somebody who's gay? You've got a wife and a kid. If you're happy with that, why should it bother you?"

*Z:* Why do you think it does?

*L:* [Pause.] Him, I think it actually does bother, but most people I think are usually just saying what they think other people expect to hear. And you can tell that sometimes, when you challenge them and they quickly acquiesce and agree to your point of view. He still wasn't willing to relent. But after a year of me challenging him every time he said anything that was antigay, I have a feeling he probably thinks I'm gay. He's probably pretty certain about it. Which, if his views are really what he feels, must be driving him nuts, because I know he respected me; he worked for and admired and liked me, and we'd go work out together and everything else. It must have driven him crazy, trying to reconcile that with his views. Which is good. Out of conflict comes growth.

*Z:* But what is there about being looked at in the shower that is so threatening?

*L:* I don't know. . . . The thought of possibly being put in . . . a position where you're not in control. Maybe it's the white man image of being in power, and sex being a way to wield that power; to actually think that somebody is willing to give up that power, or to use that power on you, challenges everything you believe. . . .

## UNASHAMED

*L:* In the Marine Corps, if there's one single theme, or counsel, that goes throughout your career, it's: "Don't disgrace the Corps." No matter what you do. You can get away with a lot, but that's one thing that is just burned into you. And again, whether that comes from people who don't want to tarnish the image, or whether you think you're held to a higher ideal. . . . Marines, we have an image and a reputation we're proud of, and we don't like to do anything that detracts from that.

*Z:* And you feel that way just as much as any other Marine.

*L:* Yeah. That doesn't mean that, pushed into a corner—If they found out I was gay, and they said, "We'll give you an option: you can resign quietly and go on your way, or you can make noise and we'll prosecute you and put you in prison," I would scream my loudest and make it as public as possible, because I know that's what the Marine Corps fears the most, and that's where my safety would lie.

There's very little I've ever been ashamed of. And I will not allow anybody to make me ashamed of being gay.

# Fired for Being Gay

by Alice Pedreira, interviewed by Mubarak S. Dahir

In 1998, social worker Alice Pedreira was fired from her job with the Kentucky Baptist Homes for Children (KBHC), a religious organization in Louisville that receives state funding to help counsel and find decent homes for troubled youth. Pedreira was open about the fact that she is a lesbian during the interview that got her the position at KBHC, but after six months on the job, she received a termination letter that stated that her lifestyle choice conflicted with the values upheld by the organization.

Pedreira filed a lawsuit with the American Civil Liberties Union (ACLU) against KBHC on the grounds that she was discriminated against due to her sexual preference. She claims that her civil rights were violated by the organization and is seeking compensation, as well as attempting to set a precedent to lessen the frequency of such occurrences for others in the future.

In the following article, Mubarak S. Dahir, a correspondent with the Boston newspaper *Bay Windows*, interviews Pedreira and her partner Nancy Goodman about the firing, their reactions, and their hopes for the outcome of the case. Pedreira is highly incensed that KBHC, a heavily state-funded organization, is using tax dollars to maintain a value system that stands in contrast to the rights guaranteed to the people of Kentucky.

The case with the ACLU is still pending, but three months after Pedreira left her job, the city of Louisville passed an ordinance forbidding city employers to discriminate against employees based on their sexual preference. However, since KBHC is considered a religious organization and not a state agency, it is exempt from the ordinance. To show their sympathy, several employees at KBHC resigned their positions on Pedreira's behalf.

*Bay Windows:* How did you ever get hooked up with the Kentucky Baptist Homes for Children [KBHC] in the first place?

*Alicia Pedreira:* I had interviewed for a special program for teenage boys with behavior disorders. I didn't get the job, but about

Mubarak S. Dahir, "Fired Lesbian Battles Government Funding of Religious Bias," *Bay Windows*, July 27, 2000. Copyright © 2000 by Mubarak S. Dahir. Reproduced by permission.

a year later, the supervisor tracked me down and asked me if I was still interested.

During the interview process, I told Jack Cox [the supervisor] that I was a lesbian. And he said, "That doesn't matter to me. I think you're the best person for the job."

Now, he did tell me there would be some reservations with some people at the central office. He told me stories about how, in the past, it had been a big to-do to hire a man who was Jewish and another man who was a Buddhist. But he said he was going to ask his boss and see what he said.

The word from Jack's boss was, yes, there might be a problem if other people found out, but it was up to Jack to hire the person he thought was best for the job.

*BW:* Why would you want that job, knowing those conditions?

*AP:* I wanted to work there because I liked teenage kids. I wanted to be under the tutelage of Jack Cox, a man who was a 25-year-veteran of social work who was well-known and well-respected. And they paid well. It was definitely the highest paying job I ever had. It paid about $10,000 a year more than the job where I was working.

## DON'T HIRE ME IF YOU'RE GOING TO FIRE ME

*BW:* Were you out at your previous job?

*AP:* Yes.

*BW:* Did you think about the difficulties of going back in the closet to work for KBHC?

*AP:* Before I was hired I told the other clinicians and my peers there that I was gay. And they even told me that they thought being gay was a great resource for them, as counselors, you know, if they ever might have to deal with a gay kid in the future. So it wasn't like I felt like this was a closeted situation.

I remember, at my interview, I told my supervisor, "Don't hire me if you're going to fire me after six months because I'm gay." And six months later, I was fired.

But it wasn't because of the people I worked with. In fact, many of them [including supervisor Jack Cox] eventually quit their jobs when I was fired. They were tremendous. I was fired by the president and vice presidents, people who had never even met me before they found out I was gay.

*BW:* How did they find out?

*AP:* Oh my God! (Takes deep breath.) It was all about a photograph.

It was August [1998], and Nance [her partner] and I had been away on vacation. I went back to work on a Monday, and that previous weekend, the Kentucky State Fair had opened.

Now, if you live outside Kentucky, this isn't going to be so apparent, but everybody goes to the State Fair. It's not just people who like pigs and chickens. Literally millions of Kentuckians go. It's a big deal.

So that Monday friends at work came up to me and said, "Do you know there's a photograph of you at the fair?"

Someone had entered this photograph taken of Nance and me the year before at the AIDS walk. I'm wearing this T-shirt of the Aegean Sea with an arrow pointing to the Isle of Lesbos, and Nance is standing behind me. We aren't doing anything sexual, but the T-shirt was a dead give-away! (Laughs.)

## PANIC AT WORK

*BW:* What did you do when you found out about the photo?

*Nance Goodman:* She called me at work and she was in a panic. She was almost incoherent. So I went down to the fair to have the photo removed. And I had this surreal conversation with the manager over the photo exhibit. She thought I was telling her they needed to take down the photo because people might think we are lesbians. She thought I was somehow ashamed. I told her—we are lesbians!

*BW:* And did they take down the photo?

*NG:* Well, they took it down, but then they put it back up. So I told them I was interested in purchasing some of the photographer's work, so they would give me his name and number. When we contacted him, he agreed to have it taken down. He felt bad.

*AP:* By then, thousands of people had seen it. Including people at work.

*BW:* But didn't they already know you were gay?

*AP:* Well, the other counselors did, but not all the staff did. One of the staffers made a complaint. He said we were sending double messages to the boys by having a lesbian work with them. But he was just the tip of the iceberg. There was already a lot of fervor going on at the central office. A week later, they asked me to resign.

Jack was crying when he told me. But I told Jack I wasn't going to resign.

## DISCRIMINATION

*BW:* Why didn't you just resign and look for another job?

*AP:* Because I felt like I hadn't done anything wrong. I told them from the beginning that I was gay. So I wasn't about to resign. I decided they were going to have to fire me. (Laughter) Which, of course, they did. . . .

The day they fired me, they took me to Dr. [William] Smithwyck's office [KBHC's president and CEO]. He said, "I just want you to know this isn't personal." And he sticks out his hand. What was I supposed to do? I just shook his hand. And at that point they gave me a statement of why I was being fired. It said my "admitted homosexuality lifestyle was not compatible with the core beliefs of Kentucky Baptist Homes for Children."

So they discriminated against me on the basis of their religious beliefs. They put it in writing.

## THE FUNDING ISSUE

*BW:* What about the argument of freedom of religion? It's their religion—shouldn't they have the right to run their institutions in accordance with their religious beliefs?

*AP:* Absolutely. But they can fund it with their own money.

The other thing is the issue of the kids who are being sent there. If parents are consciously choosing KBHC because they agree with their policies, that's one thing. But most of the kids who get sent to KBHC are sent by the state, not by parents. The state's not picking KBHC because it agrees with KBHC's religious ideas. The state is sending kids there because it is the largest available service provider.

*BW:* How do you respond to people who say that by taking money away from these organizations, you are really hurting the kids?

*AP:* I've been accused of that a lot. But part of my concern is actually for the kids who are being served by KBHC.

Can you imagine what it would be like to be a kid who's questioning his own sexual orientation and to be at KBHC? To know they don't allow any gay or lesbian staff there, and they will fire them right off the bat? How do you think it would make a kid who thinks he might be gay feel, knowing the people taking care of him believe he is immoral and sinful?

Well I can tell you what that is like, because I had a kid like that. He was 16 and bisexual. And he was scared to death. He told me, "If they are firing you, then how are they going to take care of me? Who's going to protect me?"

*BW:* What would you like to see the lawsuit accomplish?

*AP:* I would like a separation of church and state. It'd be nice if the state would not give its money to religious-based organizations that discriminate.

*BW:* Has this experience changed your life in any personal ways?

*AP:* The most personal impact it's had is to erase all internalized homophobia from within myself. On a very deep personal level, I have decided that I will always be wide open about who I am, to everybody.

# CHAPTER 5

## Marriage and Parenting

SOCIAL ISSUES FIRSTHAND

# Tying the Knot in San Francisco

by Julie and Danielle, with Steve Zimmerman

On February 12, 2004, San Francisco mayor Gavin Newsom gained national notoriety when he ordered the courts to permit same-sex marriage. The constitution of the state of California contains a clause providing equal protection for same-sex couples, and Newsom was concerned that forbidding gay marriages would be a violation of that clause. So, for nearly two weeks, he opened the doors of San Francisco City Hall to allow gay couples a place to join one another in legal wedlock.

Because many states and cities in the United States do not recognize the legality of same-sex marriage (and some forbid it outright), many gay couples are forced to settle for common-law civil unions and domestic partnerships. Thus, when San Francisco sanctioned gay marriage, same-sex partners from all over the country made the journey to the city. More than three thousand weddings took place in the weeks following the mandate until the California Supreme Court halted the process pending a lawsuit filed against the city. In August 2004, the California Supreme Court ruled that the weddings were invalid.

Julie and Danielle, a lesbian couple, were in San Francisco during the weekend of February 14, 2004. In the following article, Steve Zimmerman, a reporter for Ashland, Oregon's *Daily Tidings*, recounts the two women's legal union on February 15. Julie and Danielle tell how their decision to get married was made on the spur of the moment. The couple recognized that they had to seize the opportunity because they knew that Newsom's order could be overruled by the courts at any time. They also state that their wedding almost did not happen due to the crowd that showed up at City Hall with a similar purpose in mind.

A couple for eight years prior to tying the knot, Julie and Danielle believe that their union was worth the wait, and that performing the ceremony in front of hundreds of prospective same-

Steve Zimmerman, "Part of the Crowd in San Fran," *Ashland Daily Tidings*, February 26, 2004. Copyright © 2004 by *Ashland Daily Tidings*. Reproduced by permission.

sex newlyweds gave personal as well as public significance to their wedding.

"We were a strong couple before," Julie said over lunch, with her partner Danielle. "We have been in an eight-year monogamous relationship. But everything changed when we got married. We feel differently and our relationship is stronger and more passionate."

The Rogue Valley [Oregon] couple (who requested their last names not be used) were married on Feb. 15 [2004] one of over 700 couples married that day at city hall in San Francisco. . . .

## MAKING THE DECISION

For Julie, 36, and Danielle, 37, it was a roller-coaster ride of emotions once they decided to make the nearly six-hour drive to San Francisco.

"We heard about it on the news Wednesday . . . ," Julie said. "The next day, when I got home from work, Danielle ran into the bedroom and got the rings we had and got down on her knees and proposed. I didn't know what she was doing."

The couple, who both work in professional positions, knew they could not take off work Friday. But they knew there was a sense of urgency as the order could have been overturned in court at any time.

So, with the blessing of their employers, who gave them Monday and Tuesday off, and Julie's daughters and their boyfriends who helped with hotel reservations, the couple left on Saturday, arriving at midnight. They stayed in a hotel in Oakland and drove to city hall at 4 A.M. Sunday morning.

## HOPES ARE DASHED

When they finally arrived at city hall, they were in line with scores of others. Early in the morning, an official came out and said the 350 couples with tickets from Saturday were going to be married first. He then said only 80 of the couples in the new line would be married and the rest should go home. Not knowing what number they were, Julie and Danielle waited. They would soon find out the line stopped four couples ahead of them. They were crushed.

"I was crying so hard," Julie said. "When we got there in the morning, we were couple number 20 and now it looked like we weren't going to get married."

Later, another official came out later and told the group Julie and Danielle were in that they had a one percent chance of getting married. Others behind them had zero chance.

## THE SITUATION WORKS OUT

At 3 P.M., the one percent group was told they would indeed be married on Sunday and at 5:10 P.M., Julie and Danielle were officially pronounced spouses for life.

It was a glorious feeling that still has not ended.

"When we came out of city hall, there were people cheering and throwing rice," Danielle said. "They were sharing the moment with us and it was great celebrating our day with that many people."

The couple went to a hotel on Fisherman's Wharf for their honeymoon. When they told the desk clerk they had just been married, they were given a suite overlooking the ocean. It was the perfect end to a perfect day.

## PAST, PRESENT, AND FUTURE

Both Danielle and Julie had been married to men earlier in their lives. Julie's was a 15-year marriage, while Danielle's only lasted two years. When both decided to start new relationships, they were headed in distinctly different directions.

"I knew in elementary school I was attracted to girls," Danielle said. "I was a tomboy and had crushes on my female teachers. When I got divorced, my plan was to be with a woman."

"After my divorce, I dated one guy and then met Danielle," Julie explained. "Before I met her, I never thought I would be with a woman. It was not in my plan. But we have been together for eight years."

Julie's two daughters are very comfortable with their two moms. Her oldest daughter gave her the best piece of advice she has received.

"When I told her about our relationship, she said, 'Mom, love knows no sex.'"

The future of their union is uncertain as a court could rule the marriage invalid. But both Julie and Danielle, who are registered with Ashland's Domestic Partner Registry, say the piece of paper they received after their marriage is inconsequential.

"I am holding the same license that my ex-husband and I held when we were married," Julie noted.

"We did this because we love each other and it gives recognition to our relationship," she added. "We even did a ceremony in front of the kids. But going to San Francisco to get married finalized it for us. If it lasts for just one more day, that is fine."

# Lesbian Moms and Their Baby Boy

by Jay and Alex

Jay and Alex (pseudonyms) are a lesbian couple living in Dublin, Ireland, who decided to have a child. The pair agreed that Jay would undergo insemination from an unknown donor; however, after she failed to conceive, doctors determined that she was unable to bear children. Alex then elected to serve in the role as birth mother. A donor was chosen, and a child was conceived on the first attempt.

In the following article, Jay and Alex share their respective experiences in their new roles of motherhood. The excerpt, taken from *Coming Out: Irish Gay Experiences*, is in two parts: Alex's story and Jay's story.

In part one, Alex details her initial feelings of uncertainty regarding the prospect of adding a child to the relationship. She eventually warmed to the idea of motherhood and has since been overjoyed in raising her son. In part two, Jay gives a more introspective account of the effects of motherhood on an "out" lesbian. For herself, she recognizes that she must have a strong self image as a lesbian and a mother. For her son, she stresses how important it is for him to have a strong connection to male role models so that he can make up his own mind regarding his sexuality when he becomes old enough to understand the complexities of sexual orientation. Above all, Jay, like her partner, looks upon motherhood as a blessing.

## ALEX'S STORY

Pausing to take breath from clearing the attic—our four-month-old son is propped up on the bed watching the mayhem.

Where to begin—Jay told me she wanted a baby approximately one year after we started going out together. Not just a vague "I'm thinking about . . ." but a definite proposal. I thought it was only six months into our relationship, but I "lost" six months after my dad died, so that's how it felt. . . . We started seeing each other the same year after he died. . . . I was thirty and Jay thirty-two. She said that she wanted a baby now because she had met me. That was great to hear, but a bit perplexing too as my feelings were in a whirl.

I can't remember exactly how I felt—Jay says I was "pleased but then angry." I felt it was too early in our relationship. We went to see a couple who had had a son by donor insemination and I remember feeling quite unhappy in their kitchen. I felt like I was being bounced into a decision. Jay, once she has decided to do something, takes steps to make it happen. I live with ideas if I'm not completely moved by them. Maybe we're not that dissimilar. I just wasn't so taken with the idea.

I had talked about having children with my previous partner, but I can't remember if we ever decided who would be the birth mother—maybe we hadn't got that far. Since coming out at the age of twenty-five I always thought I would be involved with children, but not as the birth mother. Probably by meeting someone who already had children. . . .

Last August, we were in the car and I said "I want to have a baby." I'd been looking at toddlers and babies, and the phrase "I want one" kept coming into my head. Very strong and passionate feelings—overwhelmingly so. Most unusual for me, I would have said. . . .

So we began to talk again. We put an advert into a lesbian and gay paper for donors. We asked a man—a new friend. I nearly asked one of my best and oldest gay friends—well, I did ask him in a roundabout way—I asked did he know of anyone, and he said 'no'. I wanted the man to be a friend, or at least the friend of a friend. This was going to be a lifetime commitment. Jay felt the same way. . . . We understood this. I was thirty-eight by now. We both wanted to start insemination soon and I was worried that it could take one or two years for me to conceive.

After six months of looking, we decided to once again go with an unknown donor and I conceived our son at the first attempt. He is beautiful and I have never felt so much love for another human being.

There is so much more I could say—about my experience of "mothering", about our experiences as lesbian parents. Our families and friends. My feelings since the birth. Our relationship. This article is a snapshot in time, and a brief history. It by no means tells the whole story—that would take too long. . . .

## JAY'S STORY

I think I'll start by writing about the time since our son was born. We've received a huge amount of positive attention: loads of presents, offers of support, a real outpouring of what feels like love towards our child and so by implication towards us. This has been really special but I've often felt quite removed from it and like it's not really about me. I think part of me is still badly damaged by all the years of not being able to conceive. By the invisibility of that, particularly since as an infertile lesbian I belong to a not very well publicised sub-group. In fact I've never actually met anyone else of that description. So freak among freaks I'd feel on my bad days.

So my reactions to Alex announcing her intention to have a child and then very quickly, and apparently easily, producing the goods have always been mixed. I think I am mainly delighted, feeling very lucky. Certainly much luckier than straight women friends who on having found out they cannot conceive, have very few other options left whereas I had access to another whole womb.

It was a huge surprise to me when Alex said she wanted to try for a child. I'd been convinced, from everything she'd ever said, that pregnancy was not in her plans for herself. When she told me I felt terribly excited but then I cried as if my heart would break—what felt like ancient tears.

Since our son has been born I've continued to have wildly fluctuating reactions . . . veering from a quiet, pleased excitement to waves of anger, from shy pride to real panic. Sometimes I feel incredibly close to Alex and so lucky, sometimes I feel like the baby takes up a space in her life that used to be mine and I resent him (even though he is only four months old: I didn't say I would be rational here!).

I think some of the anger is around us trying to sort out our roles as parents. As one of my friends with grown-up children said to me: "Oh dear, he's going to have two Mammies!" As a couple, we've always had great battles around certain areas like DIY [do-it-yourself home improvement tasks] (who can drill the best), gardening (my great love, part of her job), cooking (she follows recipes, I don't). So I had already thought we would have some good fights ahead of us in the new arena and was anticipating them with a wry smile. However, our conflicts have actually been both more frequent and more raw than I'd imagined. It would be interesting to know if this is the case for other same sex couples. And in fact we do have straight friends who have similarly fierce arguments so maybe it's just about wanting to be an involved parent (and being stroppy).

Anyway, enough angst. Let me write about the joys and realities now! I was trying to type with the baby on my knee because he was getting a bit bored but this does not improve creativity or lucidity so he's back in the baby gym. However, I know my time is now being grudged. This is one of my days to look after the baby: we do half the week each. It is fun but I have to be very organised and often forget to take crucial things with me (nappies, teats . . . even on one horribly memorable occasion, the whole changing bag!).

At first I wanted to rush around visiting, showing him off, shopping and combining walking the dog with getting me and the baby some fresh air and exercise. After two exhausting and stressful days I realised this was not possible or sensible . . . he hated being carted around so much and I wasn't enjoying the visiting, being too concerned about his needs. The same thing was true when I took him to a work meeting: I felt vulnerable, distracted and a bit foolish. Not a good combination when trying to convince someone I am worth my money as a freelance trainer!

I am intrigued by people's reactions to him. They inevitably say: "Isn't he big?" which I finally worked out must be a compliment. They then say: "Is he good for you?" which I worked out means does he sleep all night? So I say "He's great but he doesn't sleep much"—goodness and sleep not seeming to have much to do with each other when you are talking about totally instinctive needs.

I have also been surprised at the way other lesbians address him. "He's going to be a real heartbreaker," and they mean little girls' hearts! Compulsory heterosexuality is alive and well and kicking in the lesbian community. Me and his other mum are just the same though, careful to dress him in real boy's clothes and anxious to spend time with men so he gets male role models. It's as if we feel ourselves to be out on a limb in terms of our own sexuality and are terrified that our choices will impact negatively on him, specifically in terms of his sexuality.

On my bleakest days I hope he won't be gay because the scene feels so narrow and obsessed with appearance. On my sunny, all's right with the world days, I think he'll be okay whatever he chooses to do or be. We often sing the Flirts' lullaby "You can be anybody that you want to be" to ourselves as much as to him. For of course he'll get most of his messages about the world from me and Alex these first few years so I need to keep my self-image, as a dyke, a woman and a parent, in good shape.

Invisibility does seem to be a theme in my half of this story: first my history around trying to bear a child and now my role as a . . . well, as a what? Non-biological parent, co-parent, secondary parent? Yuk! I have often been assumed to be Alex's sister or her strangely involved but extremely supportive friend. When I am with him on my own of course I am seen as his (only) mother. Which is fine unless they want to know how the birth was or am I breast-feeding him.

At different times on the same day last week I had to decide whether to come out as: a lesbian (with some young people at work), as a mother (in a taxi without the baby), and as a lesbian mother (to the older lady in the local café who thought he was my baby). Well, he is, but sometimes it's just too difficult, and often actually frightening, to have to explain.

The acuteness of this fear is new to me. I've been out for twenty years: at work, where I live, to my family. It's not always been easy, or safe, but I've only been deciding for me. Now my answers implicate our child as well, and may affect the way he is regarded and treated. . . .

Rereading this I see I have moved from my emotions before and immediately after his birth to my daily experiences as one of his mums. It's good to talk about it and, as Alex says, there is loads more we could say. It's both surprisingly ordinary and completely amazing to be living this life now. I do feel blessed and very alive.

# Why We Chose to Adopt a Child

by Dan Savage

Dan Savage is a syndicated columnist and associate editor for the *Stranger*, a Seattle-based weekly magazine. He and his partner Terry, early in their relationship, were eager to explore the world of parenthood, so they decided to bring a child into their life. In his book *The Kid*, Savage tells the entire story of how he and Terry navigated the convoluted landscape of becoming gay parents. Savage had initially attempted to become the father of a "bio-kid" with several groups of lesbians who also wanted children. Intending to serve as a co-parent, Savage made the effort to negotiate with three separate groups of women in the hopes of finding a surrogate mother who would share parental responsibilities. In each instance, the women backed out at the last minute. This left Dan and Terry with only one alternative: adoption.

In the following article, an excerpt from *The Kid*, Savage discusses the reasons why he and his partner felt the desire to be parents. Children, he says, eradicate the sense of mortality that tends to plague people once they enter the later stages of their lives. In addition, children serve to perpetuate the parents' existence by continuing on and having their own families. For Savage, children provide a much needed solution to the problem of self-fulfillment that he encountered in middle-age.

Savage also speaks frankly about the issue of whether or not he and Terry are adopting a child to prove a point. It is Savage's contention that they are indeed doing so, to a degree. He argues that in American society, the very act of holding a lover's hand in public becomes an act of significance because gays suffer incredible scrutiny from heterosexual culture. It would be impossible, thus, for Dan and Terry to adopt a child without their sexuality becoming an issue at some point in the process.

Ultimately, *The Kid* ends on a happy note, with Dan and Terry finally becoming the parents of a boy that they decide to

Dan Savage, *The Kid: What Happened After My Boyfriend and I Decided to Go Get Pregnant.* New York: Dutton, 1999. Copyright © 1999 by Dan Savage. All rights reserved. Reproduced by permission of Dutton, a division of Penguin Group (USA) Inc.

call D.J. They end up opting for the process of "open adoption," which involves maintaining an open and active relationship with the birth mother in order to keep confusion about parental roles in the child's life to a minimum. At the time the book went to print, Dan and Terry were already considering adopting a playmate for D.J.

There's a question I've been dodging.
Why were we having a kid? Or kids, plural, I should say, because Terry and I . . . believed children should have siblings to torment. So, why kids? We were HIV-negative gay men living in America at the end of the twentieth century. Barring some social or economic disaster . . . , we had a long, prosperous DINK future spread out before us. (That's "Double Income, No Kids," our by-default consumer demographic.) Remaining DINKs meant a future of travel, parties, cheap-if-not-meaningless sex, health clubs, and swank homes. Why would any gay man in his right mind trade DINKdom for dirty diapers?

"The middle age of buggers is not to be contemplated without horror," [novelist] Virginia Woolf is reported to have observed. I don't believe there's anything horrid about middle-aged gay men (provided they don't join men's choruses or the North American Man-Boy Love Association, watch *Deep Space Nine*, or display teddy bears in little leather harnesses in their living rooms). Nevertheless, at about age thirty, I began to contemplate my impending middle age with a degree of horror. What was I going to *do* for the next forty or fifty years? It didn't take me long to conclude I would need more in my life than money and men. I would want something meaningful to do with my free time, something besides traveling the world collecting Fiesta Ware and intestinal parasites.

So, kids.

## WHY HAVE A KID

Once upon a time, people had kids out of a sense of obligation to family, species, and society; and since they lacked birth control, most sexually active folks weren't in much of a position to prevent themselves from making babies. We've got birth control now, at least in most places, and we've got access to abortion, at least for now. While some couples feel pressured by their families or churches to

## MARRIAGE AND PARENTING

have kids, for a large number of people in a large part of the world, having children is optional for the first time in history. Why do people have kids today? It's not to do the species a favor: the largest threat to our survival is our out-of-control breeding. The reason people in general (by which I mean straight people, since people in general are straight) have kids today is to give themselves something real and meaningful and important to do. Having children is no longer about propagating the species or having someone to leave your lands to, but about self-fulfillment. Kids are a self-actualization project for the parents involved. . . . Something for grownups to do, a pastime, a hobby.

So why not kids? Gay men need hobbies, too.

Our other options as gay men at the end of the twentieth century—how to occupy our time over the next thirty years—were not at all appealing. Terry and I had, basically, three choices:

Option 1: Stay in the Game. Keep going to bars, and parties, and clubs, keep getting laid, keep drinking, keep taking drugs. This option leads, inevitably, to our breakup over some humpy young thing, who would in turn dump us for a humpier younger thing. Eventually we become a couple of fifty-year-old fags hanging out in gay bars full of men too young to care that we, you know, marched on Washington in '93. To compete with and compete for the annual crop of just-out twenty-one-year-old gay boys, we have to go under the knife again and again, until we are so much scar tissue stitched to scar tissue. Then we die. Our corpses, drug- and silicone-contaminated superfund sites, are denied a decent burial. Distant relatives come to town, crate us up, and haul us to a toxic-waste incinerator.

Option 2: Go Places, See Sh—. We stay together and spend our DINK dollars traveling the world. We take a lot of pictures, collect a lot of junk, have a lot of sex with the locals. Provided we don't succumb to Alzheimer's or some as-yet-undiscovered sexually transmitted disease, we have our memories to keep us company when we're old and gray. Then we die, our memories dying with us. Distant relatives come to town and haul us and everything else—photo albums, postcard collection, STD [sexually transmitted disease] meds—off to the dump.

Option 3: Mr. & Mr. Martha Stewart. We buy a house and direct the passion we used to devote to sex to the renovation and decoration of our little manse. We spend the last years of our lives combing junque stores, yard sales, estate sales, and auction houses for that authentic Victorian/Edwardian/Art Deco/Fab Fifties nightstand/hall table/mirror/dinette set that will finally complete our beautiful-but-sterile home. Once we find it, our local newspaper's Sunday magazine does a photo spread of our to-die-for home. Then we die. Distant relatives come to town, sell the house and the furniture, and donate our ancient bodies to science.

## KIDS KEEP MORTALITY AT BAY

I was already planning on having kids when I met Terry, so I'd already thought through all of this. After I walked Terry through what I saw as our options, he agreed that they were pretty depressing. Each ended with distant relatives coming to town and disposing of our remains in a tremendously unsentimental manner. And everything we would have DINKed so hard for—our possessions, our memories, our hair systems—would be busted up and thrown away. Mortality is unsettling, and the more we thought about having kids the more sense they made as hedges against depressing, lonely deaths. We didn't want to be anybody's forgotten old gay uncles.

Kids wouldn't keep us young, but they would keep us relevant, something other hobbies wouldn't do. If we had kids and they managed to outlive us, Terry and I would be hauled off to the dump when our time came by people who knew us and felt obligated to dispose of us.

So, kids.

Yes, I know: kids die, kids turn out rotten, kids grow up to be serial killers, kids abandon their parents, kids *kill* their parents. Adopted kids may decide their biological relatives are their *real* relatives and blow off their adoptive families. Kids are a crap-shoot. But even if the only thing your kids give a sh— about is getting their hands on your money or your Holden-Wakefield end tables, even if all your kids want is for you to drop dead, at least someone is giving a specific sort of sh— about you. And if you have more than one kid who wants your end tables, you can have fun drafting and redrafting your will.

## ADOPTING TO PROVE A POINT

Sometimes, late at night, I'd sit up and worry that we might be adopting to prove a point. Were we doing this because we could? On some level, I think, we were. It wasn't the sole reason, but even if we were only doing this to prove something to the world or to ourselves, there are worse reasons to have kids. Straight people all over the world have kids for those and much worse reasons every day. They fall down drunk and get up pregnant.

The same impulse that drives grown gay men to walk around holding hands could be pushing us toward this. For same-sex couples, taking a lover's hand is almost never an unself-conscious choice. You have to think about where you are, whether you're safe, and you have to look. By the time you determine you're safe, you're not even sure you want to hold hands anymore. The genuine moment has passed, but you've invested so much energy and angst that now you can't *not* take your lover's hand. You wind up holding and the only reason you take your lover's hand is to prove that you can.

Wondering whether we were doing this "just to prove we can," made us wonder about our motives. In that hesitation, the decision to adopt became more than "Let's have kids." Public displays of affection for gays and lesbians are political acts, and what could be a larger public display of affection than the two of us adopting a kid together.

# ORGANIZATIONS TO CONTACT

## AMERICAN CIVIL LIBERTIES UNION (ACLU)
125 Broad St., 18th Fl., New York, NY 10004
(212) 944-9800 • fax: (212) 869-9065
Web site: www.aclu.org

The ACLU is the nation's oldest and largest civil liberties organization. Its Lesbian and Gay Rights/AIDS Project, started in 1986, handles litigation, education, and public-policy work on behalf of gays and lesbians. The union supports same-sex marriage. It publishes the monthly newsletter *Civil Liberties Alert*, the handbook *The Rights of Lesbians and Gay Men*, the briefing paper "Lesbian and Gay Rights," and the book *The Rights of Families: The ACLU Guide to the Rights of Today's Family Members*.

## CANADIAN LESBIAN AND GAY ARCHIVES
Box 639, Station A, Toronto, ON M5W 1G2 Canada
(416) 777-2755
Web site: www.clga.ca/archives

The archives collects and maintains information and materials relating to the gay and lesbian rights movement in Canada and elsewhere. Its collection of records and other materials documenting the stories of lesbians and gay men and their organizations in Canada is available to the public for the purpose of education and research. It also publishes an annual newsletter, *Lesbian and Gay Archivist*.

## COALITION FOR POSITIVE SEXUALITY (CPS)
PO Box 77212, Washington, DC 20013-7212
(713) 604-1654
Web site: http://positive.org

CPS is a grassroots direct-action group formed in 1992 by high-school students and activists. It endeavors to counteract the institutionalized misogyny, heterosexism, homophobia, racism, and ageism that its members believe students experience at school. It is dedicated to offering teens sex education that is pro-woman, pro-lesbian/gay/bisexual, pro–safe sex, and pro-choice. Numerous pamphlets and publications are available upon request.

## COURAGE
c/o Church of St. John the Baptist, 210 W. Thirty-first St., New York, NY 10001
(212) 268-1010 • fax: (212) 268-7150
e-mail: NYCourage@aol.com • Web site: http://CourageRC.net

## ORGANIZATIONS TO CONTACT

Courage is a network of spiritual support groups for gay and lesbian Catholics who wish to lead celibate lives in accordance with Roman Catholic teachings on homosexuality. It publishes listings of local groups, a newsletter, and an annotated bibliography of books on homosexuality.

## DIGNITY/USA

1500 Massachusetts Ave. NW, Suite 8, Washington, DC 20005-1894
(800) 877-8797 • fax: (202) 429-9808
e-mail: info@dignityusa.org • Web site: www.dignityusa.org

Dignity/USA is a Roman Catholic organization of gays, lesbians, bisexuals, and their families and friends. Its members believe that homosexuals and bisexuals can lead sexually active lives in a manner consonant with Christ's teachings. Through its national and local chapters, Dignity/USA provides educational materials, AIDS crisis assistance, and spiritual support groups for members. It publishes the monthly *Dignity Journal* and a book, *Theological/Pastoral Resources: A Collection of Articles on Homosexuality from a Catholic Perspective.*

## FAMILY RESEARCH COUNCIL

801 G St. NW, Washington, DC 20001
(202) 393-2100 • fax: (202) 393-2134
Web site: www.frc.org

The council is a research and educational organization that promotes the traditional family, which the council defines as a group of people bound by marriage, blood, or adoption. The council opposes gay marriage and adoption rights. It publishes numerous reports from a conservative perspective on issues affecting the family, including *Free to Be Family.* Among its publications are the monthly newsletter *Washington Watch* and the bimonthly journal *Family Policy.*

## GAY & LESBIAN ALLIANCE AGAINST DEFAMATION (GLAAD)

5455 Wilshire Blvd., #1500, Los Angeles, CA 90036
(323) 933-2240 • fax: (323) 933-2241
Web site: www.glaad.org

GLAAD is an organization concerned with promoting fair and equal treatment of gays and lesbians in the media. Its mission is to destroy harmful stereotypes and end discrimination based on sexual orientation and gender identification. GLAAD regularly publishes media alerts and press releases to counter any media representations of gays and lesbians that the alliance believes are unfair or damaging to the gay community.

## GAY MEN'S HEALTH CRISIS (GMHC)

The Tisch Building, 119 W. Twenty-fourth St., New York, NY 10011
(212) 367-1000
Web site: http://gmhc.org

Gay Men's Health Crisis is a nonprofit organization committed to stopping the spread of the AIDS virus. Through volunteer and community support, GMHC assists people living with AIDS and seeks to improve their health and increase their independence. The main goals of GMHC are to uphold the dignity of homosexuals with the disease, fight homophobia, and offer compassion to the afflicted. The organization also strives to maintain the urgency of HIV treatment and education as a matter of national and community importance. To this end GMHC publishes annual reports on the state of the AIDS crisis in America and abroad.

## HOWARD CENTER FOR FAMILY, RELIGION, AND SOCIETY

934 N. Main St., Rockford, IL 61103
(815) 964-5819 • fax: (815) 965-1826
Web site: http://profam.org/Default.htm

The purpose of the Howard Center is to provide research and understanding that demonstrates and affirms family and religion as the foundations of a virtuous and free society. The center believes that the natural family is the fundamental unit of society. The primary mission of the Howard Center is to provide a clearinghouse of useful and relevant information to support families and their defenders throughout the world. The center publishes the monthly journal *Family in America* and the *Religion and Society Report*.

## HUMAN RIGHTS CAMPAIGN (HRC)

1640 Rhode Island Ave. NW, Washington, DC 20006
(202) 628-4160 • fax: (202) 347-5323
Web site: www.hrc.org

The HRC provides information on national political issues affecting lesbian, gay, bisexual, and transgender Americans. It offers resources to educate congressional leaders and the public on critical issues such as ending workplace discrimination, combating hate crimes, fighting HIV/AIDS, protecting gay and lesbian families, and working for better lesbian health. HRC publishes the *HRC Quarterly* and *LAWbriefs*.

## LAMBDA LEGAL DEFENSE AND EDUCATION FUND

120 Wall St., Suite 1500, New York, NY 10005-3904
(212) 809-8585 • fax: (212) 809-0055
Web site: www.lambdalegal.org

Lambda is a public-interest law firm committed to achieving full recognition of the civil rights of lesbians, gay men, and people with HIV/AIDS. The firm addresses a variety of topics, including equal marriage rights, parenting and relationship issues, and domestic partner benefits. It publishes the quarterly *Lambda Update* as well as numerous pamphlets and position papers.

## LOVE IN ACTION

PO Box 171444, Memphis, TN 38175-3307
(901) 751-2468 • fax: (901) 751-1922
Web site: www.loveinaction.org

Love in Action is a Christian ministry that believes that homosexuality is a learned behavior and that all homosexual conduct is wrong because it violates God's laws. It provides support to gays and lesbians to help them convert to heterosexuality. It also offers a residential twelve-step recovery program for individuals who have made the commitment to follow Christ and wish to leave their homosexuality behind. Current publications include a monthly newsletter.

## NATIONAL ASSOCIATION FOR THE RESEARCH AND THERAPY OF HOMOSEXUALITY (NARTH)

16633 Ventura Blvd., Suite 1340, Encino, CA 91436-1801
(818) 789-4440 • fax: (818) 789-6452
Web site: www.narth.com

NARTH is an information and referral network that believes the causes of homosexuality are primarily developmental and that it is usually responsive to psychotherapy. The association supports homosexual men and women who feel that homosexuality is contrary to their value systems and who voluntarily seek treatment. NARTH publishes the *NARTH Bulletin*, the book *Healing Homosexuality: Case Stories of Reparative Therapy*, and numerous conference papers and research articles.

## NATIONAL CENTER FOR LESBIAN RIGHTS

870 Market St., Suite 370, San Francisco, CA 94102
(415) 392-6257 • fax: (415) 392-8442
e-mail: info@NCLRights.org • Web site: www.nclrights.org

Founded in 1977, the center is an advocacy organization that provides legal counseling and representation for victims of sexual-orientation discrimination. Primary areas of advice include custody and parenting, employment, housing, the military, and insurance. The center publishes the handbooks *Recognizing Lesbian and Gay Families: Strategies for Obtaining Domestic Partners Benefits* and *Lesbian and Gay Parenting: A Psychological and Legal Perspective* as well as other materials.

## NATIONAL GAY AND LESBIAN TASK FORCE

1325 Massachusetts Ave. NW, Suite 600, Washington, DC 20005
(202) 393-5177 • fax: (202) 393-2241
e-mail: thetaskforce@thetaskforce.org • Web site: www.thetaskforce.org

The National Gay and Lesbian Task Force is a nonprofit organization involved in enhancing the political power of the lesbian, gay, bisexual, and transgendered community in order to bring about equality. The task force continually lobbies for federal and state legislation that acknowledges and defends the civil rights of gays, lesbians, bisexuals, and transgendered persons.

## PARENTS, FAMILIES, AND FRIENDS OF LESBIANS AND GAYS (PFLAG)

1726 M St. NW, Suite 400, Washington, DC 20036
(202) 467-8180 • fax: (202) 467-8194
e-mail: info@pflag.org • Web site: www.pflag.org

PFLAG is a national organization that provides support and educational services for gays, lesbians, bisexuals, and their families and friends. It works to end prejudice and discrimination against homosexual and bisexual persons. It publishes and distributes booklets and papers, including "About Our Children," "Coming Out to My Parents," and "Why Is My Child Gay?"

## RECONCILING CONGREGATION PROGRAM (RCP)

3801 N. Keeler Ave., Chicago, IL 60641
(773) 736-5526 • fax: (773) 736-5475
Web site: www.rcp.org

RCP is a network of United Methodist churches, ministries, and individuals that welcomes and supports lesbians and gay men and seeks to end homophobia and prejudice in the church and society. Its national headquarters provides resources to help local ministries achieve these goals. Among its publications are the quarterly magazine *Open Hands*, the book *And God Loves Each One*, as well as other pamphlets, studies, and videos.

## SEXUALITY INFORMATION AND EDUCATION COUNCIL OF THE UNITED STATES (SIECUS)

130 W. Forty-second St., Suite 350, New York, NY 10036-7802
(212) 819-9770 • fax: (212) 819-9776
e-mail: siecus@siecus.org • Web site: www.siecus.org

SIECUS is an organization of educators, physicians, social workers, and others who support the individual's right to acquire knowledge about sexuality and who encourage responsible sexual behavior. The council promotes comprehensive sex education for all children that includes AIDS education, teaching about homosexuality, and instruction about contraceptives and sexually transmitted diseases. Its publications include fact sheets, annotated bibliographies by topic, the booklet *Talk About Sex*, and the bimonthly *SIECUS Report*.

# FOR FURTHER RESEARCH

## BOOKS

Roslyn Banish, *Focus on Living: Portraits of Americans with HIV and AIDS*. Amherst: University of Massachusetts Press, 2003.

David Bergman, ed., *Camp Grounds: Style and Homosexuality*. Amherst: University of Massachusetts Press, 1994.

Chastity Bono and Billie Fitzpatrick, *Family Outing: A Guide to the Coming-Out Process for Gays, Lesbians, and Their Families*. Boston: Little, Brown, 1998.

Jennifer Finney Boylan, *She's Not There: A Life in Two Genders*. New York: Broadway, 2003.

Mildred L. Brown and Chloe Ann Rounsley, *True Selves: Understanding Transsexualism—for Families, Friends, Coworkers, and Helping Professionals*. San Francisco: Jossey-Bass, 2003.

Joe Dallas, *When Homosexuality Hits Home*. Eugene, OR: Harvest House, 2004.

Bob Davies and Lori Rentzel, *Coming Out of Homosexuality: New Freedom for Men and Women*. Downers Grove, IL: InterVarsity, 1993.

Rob Eichberg, *Coming Out: An Act of Love*. New York: Dutton, 1990.

Michael Galluccio, Jon Galluccio, and David Groff, *An American Family*. New York: St. Martin's Griffin, 2002.

Evan Gerstmann, *Same-Sex Marriage and the Constitution*. New York: Cambridge University Press, 2004.

Kevin Jennings, *One Teacher in Ten: Gay and Lesbian Educators Tell Their Stories*. Boston: Alyson, 1994.

Gershen Kaufman and Lev Raphael, *Coming Out of Shame: Transforming Gay and Lesbian Lives*. New York: Doubleday, 1996.

Jeff Konrad, *You Don't Have to Be Gay: Hope and Freedom for Males Struggling with Homosexuality or for Those Who Know of Someone Who Is*. Hilo, HI: Pacific, 2000.

Davina Kotulski, *Why You Should Give a Damn About Gay Marriage.* Los Angeles: Advocate, 2004.

Beth Loffreda, *Losing Matt Shepard: Life and Politics in the Aftermath of Anti-Gay Murder.* New York: Columbia University Press, 2001.

Eric Marcus, *Is It a Choice? Answers to 300 of the Most Frequently Asked Questions About Gays and Lesbians.* San Francisco: HarperSanFrancisco, 1993.

Kevin McGarry, *Fatherhood for Gay Men: An Emotional and Practical Guide to Becoming a Gay Dad.* New York: Harrington Park, 2003.

Brian McNaught, *Now That I'm Out, What Do I Do?* New York: St. Martin's, 1998.

Patrick Merla, ed., *Boys Like Us: Gay Writers Tell Their Coming Out Stories.* New York: Avon, 1996.

Marie Mohler, *Homosexual Rites of Passage: A Road to Visibility and Validation.* New York: Harrington Park, 2000.

Serena Nanda, *Gender Diversity: Crosscultural Variations.* Prospect Heights, IL: Waveland, 2000.

Leslea Newman, *Heather Has Two Mommies.* Boston: Alyson, 2000.

Barbara Perry, *In the Name of Hate: Understanding Hate Crimes.* New York: Routledge, 2001.

Michelangelo Signorile, *Outing Yourself: How to Come Out as Lesbian or Gay to Your Family, Friends, and Coworkers.* New York: Simon & Schuster, 1996.

T. Richard Sullivan, ed., *Queer Families, Common Agendas: Gay People, Lesbians, and Family Values.* New York: Harrington Park, 2000.

Jeffrey Weeks, Brian Heaphy, and Cathrine Donovan, *Same Sex Intimacies: Families of Choice and Other Life Experiments.* New York: Routledge, 2001.

Evan Wolfson, *Why Marriage Matters: America, Equality, and Gay People's Right to Marry.* New York: Simon & Schuster, 2004.

FOR FURTHER RESEARCH

# PERIODICALS

Tim Allis and Sue Carswell, "Saying It Loud," *People*, May 1993.

Rebecca T. Alpert, "Coming Out of the Closet as Politically Correct," *Tikkun*, March/April 1996.

Ginia Bellafante, "Two Fathers, with One Happy to Stay at Home," *New York Times*, January 12, 2004.

Chastity Bono, "Coming Out," *Advocate*, October 14, 1997.

Karen Breslau and Debra Rosenberg, "When a Spouse Comes Out," *Newsweek*, August 23, 2004.

Mary Elliott, "Coming Out in the Classroom: A Return to the Hard Place," *College English*, October 1996.

J. Graigory, "Does My Mom Hate Me?" *Advocate*, November 9, 2004.

Brad Knickerbocker, "Political Battles over Gay Marriage Still Spreading," *Christian Science Monitor*, November 29, 2004.

Kevin Kumala, "A Minority Within a Minority," *Advocate*, December 7, 2004.

Christopher Lisotta, "Banned in the USA," *Nation*, November 29, 2004.

Katherine Marsh, "Coming Out on Fraternity Row," *Rolling Stone*, October 26, 2000.

Lisa Neff, "The Kids Are All Right," *Advocate*, July 20, 2004.

Scott D. Ryan, Sue Pearlmutter, and Victor Groza, "Coming Out of the Closet: Opening Agencies to Gay and Lesbian Adoptive Parents," *Social Work*, January 2004.

T.A. Stewart, "Gay in Corporate America," *Fortune*, December 16, 1991.

*USA Today*, "On Marriage Battlefield, Civil Unions Offer Middle Ground," November 8, 2004.

*USA Today Magazine*, "Adoption More Open for Gays and Lesbians," April 2003.

David Usborne, "Gay with Children," *New York*, November 3, 2003.

Larry L. Walker, "The Courage to Come Out," *Essence*, March 2004.

# INDEX

AIDS/HIV, 75, 78
Alex, 108
*Almanac of American Politics (National Journal)*, 28
AZT, 76

Baldwin, Gwenn, 80
Baldwin, James, 86
Bauman, Robert, 26
Bergman, David, 86
*Beyond Acceptance: Parents of Lesbians and Gays Talk About Their Experiences* (Griffin), 12
Borhek, Mary V., 11
*Boston Globe* (newspaper), 23, 28
Breay, Doris, 24
Breay, Jim, 24
Brock, Ed, 85

Cary, Rick, 13
Clinton, Bill, 94
coming out, 9, 11, 32
  account of, 18–19
  political consequences of, 23, 26
  reactions to, 10, 36–38, 40–41
  as a teacher, 92–93
  writing about, 12–13
*Coming Out: Irish Gay Experiences* (O'Brien), 108
*Coming Out Right* (Hanson and Muchmore), 10
*Congressional Quarterly*, 28
Cox, Jack, 99
Cruz, Wilson, 80

Dahir, Mubarak S., 98
Dahmer, Jeffrey, 88
Danielle, 104
"don't ask, don't tell" policy, 94
Dowd, Gary, 12
Drinan, Robert, 24
Duplechan, Larry, 86

Fierstein, Harvey, 56
Frank, Barney, 20, 95

*Gay Face of God, The* (Simpson), 59
gay fiction, 86
gay identity, 55–57
gay narratives, 12–13
gays and lesbians
  adoption by, 114–17
  black, 88–89
Goodman, Nancy, 98
Grever, Carol, 42
Griffin, Gregory M., 12

Hanson, William, 10, 11
health care, 82–83
homophobia, 10, 38, 97
  racism and, 91–92
  among youth, 81, 89–90
homosexuality, 10, 38, 55–56

*In Living Color* (TV series), 88

Jack, 35
Jay, 108
John Paul II (pope), 24
Julie, 104
*Just Above My Head* (James Baldwin), 86

*Kid, The* (Savage), 113
Kramer, Larry, 56
Kushner, Tony, 56

Lade, Alison, 67
Lincoln, Abraham, 25
Liston, Carol, 23
Longcope, Kay, 21, 28
Luke, 94

Manochio, Anthony, 61
marriage, same-sex, 104
McDougall, Bryce, 40
Media Project, 80
Mills, Anna, 50
Mixner, David, 95
Morris, David, 75
Moses, Herb, 21, 28–29
Muchmore, Wes, 10, 11

*National Journal*, 28

Newsom, Gavin, 104
Noble, Elaine, 23

O'Brien, Glen, 108
O'Neill, Tip, 26

Peabody, Daniel, 30
Pedreira, Alice, 98
PFLAG (Parents and Friends of Lesbians and Gays), 33
*Politics of America (Congressional Quarterly)*, 28
Preston, John, 13

Roth, Jordan, 54

Savage, Dan, 113
sexual preference, 54–55
Simpson, Bruce J., 59
Smithwyck, William, 101

Thorne, Tracy, 95

Wells, Jase, 16
Woolf, Virginia, 114

Zeeland, Steve, 94
Zimmerman, Steve, 104